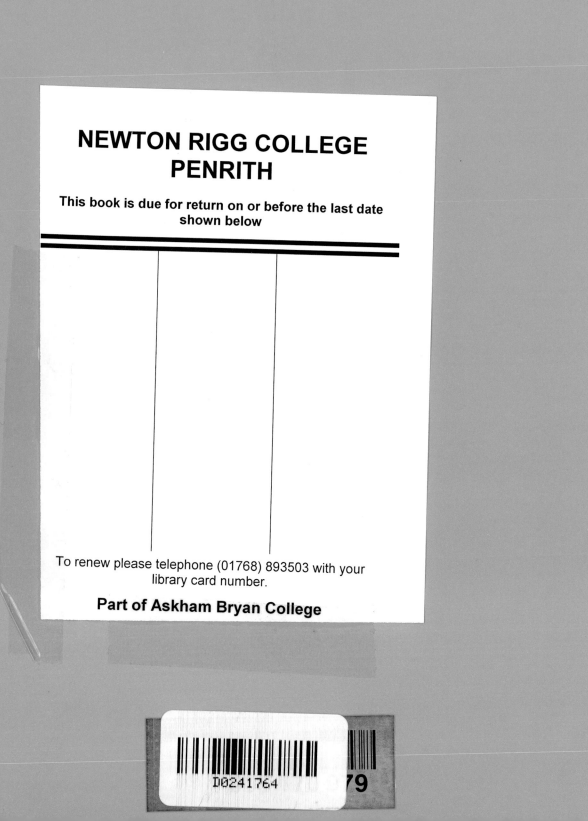

NEWTON RIGG COLLEGE PENRITH

This book is due for return on or before the last date shown below

To renew please telephone (01768) 893503 with your library card number.

Part of Askham Bryan College

MILLER'S

GARDEN ANTIQUES

HOW TO SOURCE & IDENTIFY

MILLER'S

GARDEN ANTIQUES

HOW TO SOURCE & IDENTIFY

RUPERT VAN DER WERFF
& JACKIE REES

MILLER'S GARDEN ANTIQUES

RUPERT VAN DER WERFF & JACKIE REES

First published in Great Britain in 2003 by Miller's,
an imprint of Octopus Publishing Group Ltd,
2–4 Heron Quays, London, E14 4JP

Miller's is a registered trademark of Octopus Publishing Group Ltd

Commissioning Editor	Anna Sanderson
Executive Art Editor	Rhonda Fisher
Project Editor	Emily Anderson
Designer & Illustrator	Vicky Short
Jacket Design	Victoria Bevan
Editor	Claire Musters
Proofreader	Laura Hicks
Indexer	Sue Farr
Production	Angela Couchman
Special Photography	Glynn Clarkson

The publishers will be grateful for any information that will assist them in keeping future
editions up to date. While every care has been taken in the preparation of this book, neither
the author nor the publisher can accept any liability for any consequence arising from the use
thereof, or the information contained therein.

ISBN 1 84000 713 3

A CIP catalogue record for this book is available from the British Library

Set in Fruitger, Novarese, and Trajan
Produced by Toppan Printing Co., (HK) Ltd.
Printed and bound in China

Front Cover (clockwise from top left): cast-iron latticed seat, late 19th century, £2,000–3,000/$3,000–4,500; zinc egret
fountain, American, c.1900, £2,000–3,000/$3,000–4,500; white-marble sundial, c.1900, £1,200–1,800/$1,800–2,700;
stoneware urn, c.1865, £800–1,200/$1,200–1,800; wooden side gate, Edwardian, early 20th century, £300–500/$450–750

Back Cover: top: hedge clipper, Ridgeways, c.1890–1920, £40–60/$60–90; bottom: sheet-metal weather vane,
20th century, £400–600/$600–900

Half-Title: bronze urn, French, late 19th century, £4,000–6,000/$6,000–9,000

Contents: bronze figure of Mercury after the original by Giam Bologna, late 19th century, £6,000–10,000/$9,000–15,000

CONTENTS

INTRODUCTION

The garden is a haven of tranquillity in a stressful world, and deserves as much attention as the decorations within a home. When waking up on a summer morning, with the sun just rising and dew on the grass, look out of your window and try to imagine what you would like to see: perhaps a figure of a Venus half hidden in the bushes or a row of urns planted with flowers. There is a wealth of garden statuary and ornament and it is possible to achieve the look you want without breaking the bank.

Garden ornament is an area of increasing interest, fuelled by the many television programmes about gardening and even more about antiques. This keen interest means that there are many outlets for garden ornament, so it is both affordable and easily available. The popularity of antique statues, seats, urns, and fountains has never waned, and the market for these has risen steadily over the last 15 years. This book provides information on all garden ornament, as well as listing the possible pitfalls in each area. The focus is on "affordable" ornaments so most of the pieces illustrated date from the 19th century or later.

During the Industrial Revolution the Victorian middle classes began to emulate the decorative style that had previously been the preserve of the great landowners. This led to an enormous growth in the manufacture of ornamentation during the mid- to late 19th century and a surge of interest in such items began to occur in the USA too. Of course you cannot expect to recreate in your back garden the ornament found in the grounds of famous English country houses, but you can find cast-stone copies of antique statuary at a fraction of the price of an original. It is also possible to purchase Victorian cast-iron garden furniture and urns, as well as find modern copies.

A well-placed modest piece will always look better than a badly displayed piece of better quality, and the garden offers great scope for design and imagination. We hope that this book will help you to investigate all the possibilities for garden ornament and furniture in your own garden space.

MATERIALS

Garden ornaments have always been produced in a wide range of materials – stones, marbles, metals, ceramics, and composites. The earliest ornaments were carved from stone or marble; stoneware and terracotta came much later, from the late 18th century onwards. It is useful to understand which material would work best on any chosen site, so that the ornament you buy is exactly right for its situation. The following list will help you identify all the different materials and give some guidance as to their advantages, as well as their drawbacks, to assist you when making your purchase.

MARBLE

▲ **Good-quality statuary marble**

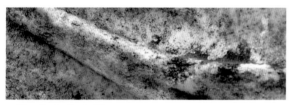

▲ **Weathered marble**

▲ **Rosso Verona**

▲ **Istrian marble**

The use of marble for garden ornament has a long history. The surface that can be achieved with good-quality marble has endeared it to artists since the earliest times. Marble is a metamorphic rock formed by limestone that has been heated and pressurized in the Earth's crust. It can be found in an enormous variety of colours, which is another reason why it has always been so highly prized.

Good-quality statuary marble
This pure white marble has a smooth, almost shiny, finish and is how marble should look. However, in colder climates the surface of the marble will abrade unless the statuary is kept covered during the winter. In warm climates, such as in Italy, the marble will retain its smooth surface even if kept outside.

Weathered marble
The photograph shows what happens to the surface of statuary marble if it is exposed to cold weather. When marble weathers the surface loses its brilliant smoothness and gradually erodes until it resembles a sugar cube. If nothing is done to prevent damage the only remedy will be to recarve the piece, which causes a loss of originality and value.

Rosso Verona
This is a pinkish-red marble found in the area around Verona in north-east Italy. The marble deepens to a pinkish-red when it is wet and for this reason was often used for wellheads and wall-fountains.

Istrian marble
Often referred to as marble, this is really a kind of granite and it can be found carved into all manner of garden ornaments. A great many neo-Roman reproduction figures are made of this material.

STONE

▲ **Gritstone**

▲ **Portland stone**

▲ **Bath stone**

▲ **Limestone**

▲ **Vicenza stone**

Stone encompasses a huge variety of materials, many of which have been used for garden ornament. The weathering of stone is one of its likeable qualities, and the array of mosses and lichens that can grow on it often adds to a piece's beauty. Think carefully before you clean a stone item as you may be destroying more of its value than you realize.

Gritstone

This is an extremely hard stone, found in the Low Countries, and it is incredibly difficult to carve. Examples of garden ornament made of this material are scarce, but have the advantage that they will never crumble with bad weather and the carving will remain crisp for hundreds of years.

Portland stone

Portland stone is a whitish limestone from Dorset and is perhaps the most famous stone to be used in the UK. When the Houses of Parliament were restored by Sir Charles Barry and his associate, Pugin, after the fire that destroyed the House of Commons in the middle of the 19th century, all the replacement carvings were made of Portland stone.

Bath stone

A yellowish-grey stone quarried near Bath, England, this is Middle Jurassic Oolite and is the stone that gives the golden glimmer to the graceful crescents in Bath. Owing to its warm colour it is particularly effective in northern countries.

Limestone

This whitish soft stone is finely textured so ornaments made from it can incorporate intricate detailing. Limestone is the softest of all quarried stone and was used extensively in the 19th and 20th centuries. It does weather quickly, so detailing is lost over a period of time if it is unprotected from climatic extremes.

Vicenza stone

A soft Italian limestone, Vicenza stone is porous and will weather quickly, so you will get that sought-after mossy look after just a few years. The popularity of Vicenza is due to the fact that it is very easily carved when freshly quarried, which makes it much cheaper than harder stones.

COMPOSITION STONE

▲ **Pieces of aggregate in composition stone**

Composition stone is a wet mix of ground-up stone combined with various aggregates – basically a kind of concrete. It depends on the mix as to whether there are large or small pieces of aggregate in the stone. Composition stone is sometimes called "cement fondue", "cast stone", or "moulded stone". The thing to remember is that it is made in a mould, and therefore the piece you are looking at is unlikely to be unique.

TERRACOTTA

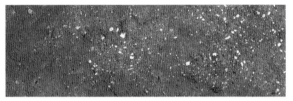

▲ **Terracotta**

▲ **Decoration on a Compton Pottery urn**

Terracotta, which literally means "fired earth", encompasses a wide variety of materials. For the garden these break down to terracotta, a clay-based material that is fired at a relatively low temperature and is not suited to the British climate; fireclay – the material that fireclay bricks are made of is fired to a higher temperature and so is much more resilient; and stoneware, which in addition to clay has crushed flint and glass in the mix. This last material is fired to such a high temperature that it semi-vitrifies, making it practically weatherproof. The colour can vary from reddish brown to a pale cream, depending on the mix and how much oxygen was present during the firing. Terracotta was one of the earliest materials produced by man, and the plastic property of the material before it is fired enables a fantastic variety of shapes and products to be made. The use of terracotta in the garden will be familiar to everyone owning a humble plant pot, but it can also be a lot more sophisticated.

CAST IRON

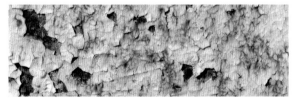

▲ **Layers of old paint on cast iron**

There is always some confusion between cast iron and steel. Technically, the difference is just a few per cent in the carbon content of the material, and for all but the absolute purists the term cast iron suffices for both.

Layers of paint
Many layers of old paint can be seen in the picture here. Before the development of zinc-based coatings, which stopped cast iron rusting, it was necessary to paint garden pieces frequently. Unless it has been stripped completely, an old piece should therefore have several layers of old paint on it.

BRONZE

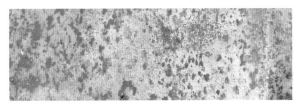

▲ **Bronze patina**

▲ **"Fake" bronze patina**

Bronze was one of the first alloys to be used, and its history can be traced back to before the third millennium BC. It is an alloy of copper and tin; the precise proportions are not exact and there are normally several other trace elements in the mix as well. The use of bronze in art is well known, and an exceptional level of skill was developed long ago in the making of Roman and Greek bronzes. Bronze can be confused with brass, as they look very similar, but few items were made in brass for the garden.

Bronze patina

You can tell bronze by its golden colour and by the way it develops a wonderful patina when left outside. The patina varies according to where the bronze has been kept, but it is normally mid- to light green in colour.

"Fake" or artificially aged bronze patina

Patinas can be artificially created, and for centuries forgers have been inventing ways of producing fake ones. A genuine patina will be hard and look as if it is part of the piece; artificial ones tend to be powdery or too light in colour.

LEAD

▲ **Weathered lead patina**

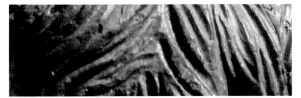

▲ **Modern leadwork**

Lead's softness and low melting temperature have ensured that it has had a long history of use. The Romans used lead widely for such diverse things as coinage and plumbing. Lead was also described by the English garden designer and writer Gertrude Jekyll as being the most suitable material for garden ornament in the British climate as it is weather resistant.

Weathered lead patina

Over the course of time lead develops a patina that, once seen, can never be mistaken for a modern imitation. However, it does have its drawbacks: its heavy weight and softness mean that buckling can occur – it is common to see urns with partly collapsed feet. The use of lead for figural work presents the biggest problems, and inside most large-scale works there is an iron armature to support the weight.

Modern leadwork

Good leadwork is extremely sought after and so prices can be high. Copies made in the 20th century, by firms such as Crowthers or the Bulbeck Foundry, go a long way towards recapturing the beauty of 18th-century leadwork at a fraction of the price, and should not, therefore, be disregarded because of their young age.

GATES & ENTRANCE WAYS

Since the earliest times people have sought to protect their properties with walls and fences. Gates developed as a practical means of maintaining easy access and yet still providing security. During the 16th century the development of effective artillery made castles and other fortified strongholds largely obsolete, and this led to the rise of bronze, iron, and wooden gates as the most efficient methods by which to secure dwellings. Gates from the 17th and 18th centuries are relatively rare and command a considerable premium. The 19th century offers the best range of suitable gates, as the majority still cost far less than modern equivalents, and will maintain their value.

Georgian gates are usually more simple and graceful than their Victorian counterparts, which usually have many decorative embellishments. Georgian gates tended to be made of wrought iron, hand-crafted by a local blacksmith, whereas from the mid-19th century gates were usually manufactured in cast iron. The gateway was the first part of the house to be seen by visitors and, in both Georgian and Victorian times, gates were seen as a key way to demonstrate a person's prosperity.

Using gates for security purposes was far more important in America, where law and order was hard to maintain outside the cities, than in Europe. In the late 17th and early 18th centuries gates and fences in America were mostly made of stone or wood and it was not until a century later that the intricate cast- and wrought-iron gates popular in Europe became available in America.

This chapter illustrates the great variety of gates on the market today. So many big houses have been demolished to make room for smaller housing estates that original gates have often been sold off to salvage yards, or offered for sale at auction. Big carriage-drive gates are at a premium so are usually still expensive. If you are looking for a bargain, consider gates with a monogram, initials, or even a house name on them. These panels can be replaced with another design, often for less than the cost of a plainer example.

CAST & WROUGHT IRON

The durability of cast and wrought iron has ensured that most gates are made of this material. The advantages are obvious – it cannot easily be cut through and will not rot, there is a vast variety of design, and antique gates are easy to obtain. As large houses are broken up into separate units, or demolished altogether, the gateways are removed and, in most instances, will find their way to an architectural salvage yard, an antiques dealer, or an auction house. Owing to the large number of gates available, and the small number of purchasers, prices for antique gates remain reasonable.

◀ **A pair of rare wrought-iron gates, late 17th century**
This wrought iron has been hammered by an estate blacksmith, the barley twist uprights twisted in different directions so that the opposing pairs match. At first glance these gates appear very similar to 19th-century examples, but on closer inspection it's possible to detect the hammer blows on each component. It is most unusual to find intact 17th-century wrought-iron work.
£4,000–5,000/$6,000–7,500

This shows how collar-tied scrolls make up a gate panel.

◀ **A pair of wrought-iron gates, late 19th century**
These gates have a multitude of decorative collar-tied scrolls, but are also functional as the lower sections have cross bars that would prevent animals or children from escaping through the gates.
£2,000–3,000/$3,000–4,500

▲ **A pair of cast- and wrought-iron gates,** *c.*1870
Wide enough for a car, these gates have shield-shaped central finials to hold a coat-of-arms, or a house name or number.
£3,000–5,000/$4,500–7,500

▲ **Coalbrookdale cast-iron gate,** *c.*1880
This side gate is stamped with the Coalbrookdale name so it has a higher value than a similar gate that is unmarked. However, side gates generally do not attain high prices at auction. **£300–500/$450–750**

▲ **Late Victorian high-quality cast- and wrought-iron gates**
These impressive gates were made originally for Smithfield Fruit and Vegetable Market, Birmingham, by Hart, Son, Peard & Co. They are typical of the high-quality workmanship you can expect from foundries that were producing at the end of the 19th century.
£7,000–8,000/$10,500–12,000

GATES

● Manufacturers of wrought- and cast-iron gates can reproduce a gate from a photograph or drawing but this is quite expensive. Consider buying old gates and having them restored or altered; it is sometimes more cost effective to alter the gate-posts to accommodate a new gate than vice versa.

● Check that the width of the gate allows easy access to all kinds of vehicles. Some Victorian gates were designed for pedestrian access only, and carriage-drive gates are too large for most modern homes. Side gates are much easier as their size has never altered significantly.

● Condition is key: Victorian or Edwardian iron gates nearly always have some rust or damage, but missing pieces can be replaced, and rust removed by spot-blasting. The gates should be cleaned of old paint, zinc-plated, and then painted in your chosen colour. If you are not keen on tackling the problem yourself there are "Blast Treating" companies who specialize in this kind of work.

● Be careful to check wooden gates for poor maintenance – any damp or rotten framework will entail extensive repairs and restoration.

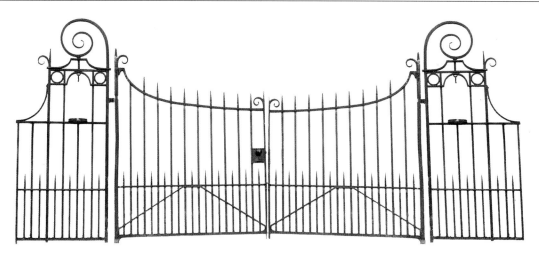

▲ **A wrought-iron gateway, early 20th century**
This design is typical of the kind of gate that was popular in the early part of the 20th century, being functional as well as decorative. However, these particular gates would not be very suitable for use where security is a major consideration, as the bars are very widely spaced.
£2,000–3,000/$3,000–4,500

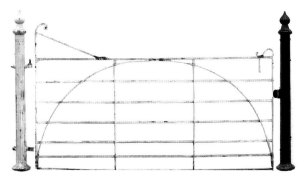

▲ **A wrought-iron estate gate, late 19th century**
Such plain, elegant estate gates are much sought after today, as they are wide enough to allow access to a car but also have a charming simplicity of style.
£800–1,200/$1,200–1,800

◀ **A pair of cast- and wrought-iron gates, French, 19th century**
These are typical of the kind of gates popular in France. French gates invariably have a solid lower section (useful for keeping children and animals from running onto roadways), and these impressive gates also have an ornate scrolling overthrow with a stylized star at the centre. **£2,000–3,000/ $3,000–4,500**

▲ **Pair of white wrought- and cast-iron gates, French, late 19th century**
These gates would be easier to fit into a modern gateway than the previous example. As old houses in France are being replaced with modern homes a quantity of these French gates have come onto the market. **£1,000–1,500/$1,500–2,250**

WOODEN GATES

Most wooden gates in existence today date to the early part of the 20th century as it is unlikely that an earlier gate would have survived. The value in 20th-century gates lies chiefly in the design and depends upon popular taste. Although you may be tempted to repaint an early wooden gate its original condition of flaking old paint does in fact add to its value. When buying wooden gates look at the bottom bar – these have been in contact with the ground so there are likely to be areas of decay.

▲ **A pair of painted oak gates, early 20th century**
This type of design is very popular today, as the gates are large enough to use as driveway gates, but the styling is simple and non-pretentious.
£500–700/$750–1,050

▲ **A wooden gate, early 20th century**
This gate is wide enough for use on a driveway and is of an attractive, rustic design. It is also in good condition.
£500–700/$750–1,050

▲ **A wooden side gate, Edwardian, early 20th century**
Suitable for a front path or the gateway into a paddock or orchard, this type of design is much sought after today.
£300–500/$450–750

FINIALS & URNS

The first question to be addressed is, "What is the difference between an urn and a finial?". The answer is that it is sometimes difficult to tell from the outside shape, but an urn is hollow and can hold something, while a finial is closed and solid. Urns can therefore be planted out whereas finials are purely decorative pieces in their own right.

The gateways of grand houses in earlier centuries were often set with carved stone finials depicting the coat-of-arms of the family, or with animals associated with them. A more modest finial would be a plain gatepier ball or a pair of pineapples. The pineapple was widely used in the 17th and 18th centuries as it represented "welcome" to visitors – a more permanent welcome than simply having the word printed on your doormat.

Urns are perhaps the most common form of garden decoration today, and if you are looking for an antique urn there is a vast variety from which to choose. They come in a range of materials: marble, lead, stone, composition stone, bronze, terracotta, and cast iron. The earliest examples were marble or stone ones, hand-carved by a local craftsman or imported from Italy by the sons of wealthy families when they ventured abroad on the "Grand Tour".

In the 18th and 19th centuries copies of famous antique originals, such as the Warwick Vase and the Medici and Borghese urns, all found their way to England in large numbers (and later to North America), and were also copied. It is possible to obtain such models in both cast iron and composition stone.

Many modern gardens have an urn as part of the decorative scheme, usually planted out but sometimes used as a fountain or a finial. It is quite easy to adapt a large urn for use as a fountain; the urn body is usually separate from the foot, so a pipe can be put up the centre of the urn from beneath. If you put the urn on a pedestal then the water container and the pump can be hidden inside the pedestal. Composition stone urns are very affordable and should weather quickly so that they look old; however, they will not increase in value in the same way that an antique urn will.

MARBLE

The material marble has always been highly esteemed and seen as something of a status symbol. The famous antique urns, such as the Warwick Vase and the Medici and Borghese urns, were all made of marble. A marble urn will add a great deal to your garden design, but will need a little care so that it does not become damaged during the frosts of winter. As water expands when it freezes, you do not want the urn full of wet earth during the winter; you need to empty it and protect it from sub-zero temperatures. Marble is quite soft, so even gentle brushing can scar the surface and cause aesthetic and financial damage; a pressure washer carefully applied (just using water) is the best method. If the piece is valuable consult an expert restorer. Never be tempted to use bleach to whiten stained marble.

▲ **White marble planter, Italian, 18th century**
Here the surface of the marble is weathered and abraded, which reduces the overall value significantly – if it was in perfect condition it would be worth twice as much.
£2,000–3,000/ $3,000–4,500

Weathering has caused the marble to become discoloured and the surface abraded.

▲ **Small, white, campana-shaped marble urn, late 19th century**
This urn is possibly French because of the high-waisted body and bulbous lower half – a design popular in France in the 19th century. Designs produced for the English market were more attenuated and elegant.
£500–800/$750–1,200

▲ **A campana-shaped white marble urn, Italian, 20th century**
This simple shape is perhaps the most effective. Note the waisted body and the outswept rim; this is more elegant than the example on page 20 and shows the difference between French and English taste. **£1,000–1,500/$1,500–2,250**

▲ **A white marble copy of the Warwick Vase, Italian, 19th century**
This is an example of a copy of an original antique; copies like this were produced in Italy to feed the European market. Such items were, and still are, extremely popular. Note the crispness of the beaded rim of this piece.
£5,000–8,000/$7,500–12,000

THE WARWICK VASE

The marble original of this vase was discovered in Herculaneum in 1771. It was purchased by Sir William Hamilton and sold after restoration to the Earl of Warwick, who for a long time forbade casts to be made of it. Eventually the Italian engraver Giovanni Piranesi (born in the early 18th century) was permitted to produce engravings of the vase and, based on these, bronze and cast-iron replicas were made and copied, on a reduced scale, in silver, bronze, and terracotta. It is perhaps the most famous antique vase after the Borghese and Medici urns.

STONE

Carved stone ornaments have been a part of English gardens since the 15th century and many of the traditional designs popular then are still used, in updated versions, today. The size of the granules that make up a stone dictate how finely it can be carved – stones such as Caen stone and limestone are so fine that the detail that can be carved into them is astonishing. Some stones, like Bath stone, are soft and require looking after while harder ones, like granite, are almost indestructible.

▲ **A pair of George III carved Neo-classical sandstone finials**, *c.*1780
These finials, which have tasselled drapes carved into them, are originally from an 18th-century gateway, where they would have been set up on gatepiers.
£2,500–4,000/$3,750–6,000

▶ **One of a pair of limestone finials, French, late 18th/early 19th century**
This design, with its draped top, was often called a "funerary urn" and would have been used as a memorial. Although well carved, it is rather gloomy for modern tastes.
£1,000–1,500/ $1,500–2,250

▲ **One of a pair of Victorian sandstone gatepier finials**, *c.*1870
Typical of the Victorian Gothic style, these substantial finials would need to be set on similarly substantial gateposts.
£800–1,200/$1,200–1,800

◀ **A pair of carved stone planters, French, 19th century**
These are perhaps rather heavy for modern taste, and for this reason are affordable in today's market. They are made of a very fine-grained stone and should withstand the northern European climate well.
£2,000–3,000/$3,000–4,500

▲ **A pair of carved Vicenza finials, Italian, late 20th century**
These are examples of the wealth of ornament still being produced today in the area around Venice. Although they are modern pieces they will weather quickly, and in a few years will look as if they have been around for decades.
£3,000–5,000/$4,500–7,500

◀ **A sandstone urn, late 19th century**
This urn, which was once magnificent, has suffered considerable weathering and some losses, so it is relatively "cheap" to buy. This damage may appeal to a modern buyer who can recognize the intricacy of the carving and may value the weathering as proof of its age. However, in pristine condition it would be worth three times as much. **£400–600/$600–900**

COMPOSITION STONE

Garden ornament has been manufactured in composition stone for centuries, but the majority of pieces were produced from the late 19th century onwards and are still being made today. It is sometimes difficult to tell the difference between carved stone and composition, especially if the ornament has become weathered. One thing to look for is little bubbles on the surface; composition stone is a wet mix and when it is being made small bubbles occur that break when the mix is setting.

Although composition stone is resistant to frosts, it is brittle and can be damaged if knocked. These petals are particularly susceptible to such damage.

▲ **An Austin and Seeley composition-stone jardiniere, late 19th century**
This is an elegant design, and despite the damage to the edges of the top petals it remains a valuable object.
£2,500–4,000/$3,750–6,000

▲ **Cast-stone urn, French, 20th century**
Although this is a more modern example, the design dates to the 18th century. This particular urn is absolutely enormous, standing more than 1.8m (6ft) high.
£3,000–5,000/$5,000–7,500

▲ **Two composition-stone planters, 20th century**
These are made to look like sections of tree trunk and are quite effective when planted out. Items that are unusual and decorative like these can be quite expensive.
£250–300/$375–450 each

▲ **Composition-stone finial, late 20th century**
Known as "The Pope Urn", this is an example of how composition stone can weather and look almost as good as carved stone in the right settings. This finial dates to the latter part of the 20th century but has weathered during the last 20 years to look ten times its age.
£600–1,000/$900–1,500 (if weathered)

▲ **A small composition-stone urn, French, 20th century**
Although made in the early 20th century, this piece is based on an 18th-century design. The composition material has been stained with pink so that the urn resembles terracotta. It is a good and decorative casting and, although it is neither carved stone nor terracotta, the design makes it a desirable piece.
£250–350/$375–525

◀ **A composition-stone pinecone finial, 20th century**
Such finials are very popular and can be found in many materials. Their popularity lies in the fact that they fit in with most gateways, and can be obtained in several sizes. This very satisfying design based on a pine cone, like similar pineapple finials, is produced in composition stone by various manufacturers and is very reasonable in price.
£200–300/$300–450

TERRACOTTA & STONEWARE

The advantage of terracotta and stoneware is that they can be moulded; identical pieces can then be made cheaply once the pattern is produced. The Coade factory of Lambeth, in the late 18th and early 19th centuries, arguably produced the finest stoneware ornament, but there is a wealth of lesser factories that also produced good items, and all are very collectable today. Both materials are fired clay but stoneware is fired at a higher temperature, which makes it more durable and allows for finer detail.

◄ **Basketweave terracotta planters, mid- to late 19th century**
These planters are particularly appealing to modern taste. The cream-coloured planters on the top row are by J.M. Blashfield, and are stamped "J M Blashfield, Stamford Pottery, Stamford", while the red ones are by the Weston Super Mare Royal Pottery and are stamped "John Matthews, Late Phillips Royal Pottery, Weston Super Mare".
£300–3,000/$450–4,500 (each)

CONDITION OF TERRACOTTA & STONEWARE

The value of terracotta is very much dictated by its condition. Breaks are hard to restore well, and surface flaking seriously detracts from a piece's value. In addition, the black grime that arises from air pollution near industrial or urban complexes can be hard to clean, so if it offends your eye think twice about buying a piece. Fireclay (a type of terracotta) and stoneware are both impervious to water so are relatively easy to look after. The areas that require attention are those where water can collect, and if there is a risk of frost it is prudent to dry or protect pieces in order to avoid such damage.

▲ **Doulton terracotta planter, c.1900**
This is one of a pair and is stamped "Doulton and Co Ltd., Lambeth", which adds to its value. There is an Art Nouveau feel to such planters and this is typical of designs made at the time.
£600–1,000/$900–1,500 (the pair)

The Manifattura di Signa mark – these stamps are small so can be missed.

▲ **A stoneware copy of the Townley Vase, mid-19th century**

The original vase was dug up at Monti Cagnolo near Rome in the 18th century and dates back to the 2nd century AD. This copy has no manufacturer's stamp but is a design widely used by many terracotta producers. **£1,200–1,800/$1,800–2,700**

▲ **A terracotta bowl on a stand, Italian, early 20th century**

This design was based on the finds of Roman furniture at Herculaneum and Pompeii. It was made by an Italian company called Manifaturra di Signa, which specialized in this Classical, very decorative design. **£3,000–5,000/$4,500–7,500**

LIBERTY & CO.

At the start of the 20th century Liberty & Co. commissioned a range of terracotta garden planters from various different manufacturers. Of particular note was a range decorated with Celtic designs, made by the Potters Art Guild (*see* page 28). All of these pieces were Arts and Crafts in style, and they have since become classics of garden design.

◀ **Selection of Compton Pottery planters, early 20th century**

The top planter is a Compton Pottery "snake pot", so-called because of the decoration around the neck. The other planters – decorated with Celtic designs – were made by the Compton Pottery and retailed through Liberty & Co. These pots are very popular today and attract high prices. **£1,000–1,500/ $1,500–2,250 (each)**

COMPTON POTTERY

The Compton Potters Art Guild was started by Mary Watts, wife of the painter George Watts. In 1895 work began on the Watts Mortuary Chapel as a memorial to George. Designed by Mary, it was to be built from local clay by the villagers of Compton. The Watts had been supporters of the Home Arts and Industries Association, a movement launched by Earl Brownlow in 1885 to revive the art of handicrafts among the working classes. The idea was that uneducated artisans should have their eyes opened to the wonders of art, and be rescued from idleness, gambling, and drinking. The standard of craftsmanship in Mary's new evening class was such that, after the exterior of the chapel was complete, it was able to turn professional. Initially known as Compton Terracotta Home Arts, it became the Compton Potters Art Guild and went on to win medals at the Chelsea Flower Show, the Royal Botanical Society, and the Home Arts' highest achievement – the gold cross. The Guild received architectural commissions from Lutyens, Clough William-Ellis, and Goodhart Rendel. Made a limited company in 1936, the Guild continued to produce works based on Mrs Watts' designs, even after her death in 1938, until the mid-1950s.

▲ **"Scroll pot" by Compton Pottery, early 20th century**
This design was much favoured by Gertrude Jekyll, so much so that it is sometimes known as the "Jekyll pot". The pot comes in five sizes, ranging from 25cm to 56cm (9¾–22in), and the Potters Art Guild stamp should be visible on the outside of the shoulder. **£1,000–1,500/$1,500–2,250**

The look of weathered patina is popular, and therefore adds value.

▶ **A stoneware urn, c.1865**
There is no visible stamp on this urn but the quality of the moulding and the finish of the stoneware make it very likely that this was made by Blanchard. It has the slightly weathered look that is favoured by English buyers, and which increases the urn's value.
£800–1,200/$1,200–1,800

◄ **Blashfield stoneware urn, *c*.1880**
The moulding is still crisp and the detail of the masks on the upturned loop handles is still very clear. The urn also has its manufacturer's stamp so it is worth more.
£1,000–1,500/$1,500–2,250

This highlights the quality of the modelling – the masks are as crisp today as they were when the urn first came out of the mould in the 19th century.

◄ **A pair of Pulham stoneware urns, late 19th/early 20th century**
These urns have been stamped "Pulhams Terracotta, Broxbourne". This particular design is known as "The Oxford Vase" and was innovative at the time. The high-shouldered, classical shape and overscroll handles are a move away from the more traditional double-handled campana.
£1,500–2,500/$2,250–3,750 (the pair)

BRONZE

Since the Italian Renaissance bronze has been a popular material in the production of garden ornament. When exposed to the northern climate it takes on an attractive green/brown patina. It is an expensive material, and the production costs of bronze urns in Europe has resulted in a ready market for resin replicas. With the naked eye it is quite difficult to spot these, but bronze rings when you tap it whereas resin has a dull sound. Bronze is also heat resistant, while resin melts far more readily.

▲ **A bronze model of the Warwick Vase, late 20th century**
This is a good example of a bronze reproduction of the marble original because the detail is sharp and the casting crisp.
£2,000–3,000/$3,000–4,500

▲ **A bronze urn, French, late 19th century**
This bronze urn is a copy of an original believed to have been cast by Duval from designs by Claude Ballin. The Ballin originals can still be found today on the short marble plinth that separates the Parterre du Nord from the Parterre d'Eau in Versailles.
£4,000–6,000/$6,000–9,000

▶ **Bronze urn, French, late 19th century**
The design of this bronze urn was taken from an original designed by Claude Ballin, Louis XIV's goldsmith, which is in the gardens of Versailles. More modern copies of such urns are also now appearing on the market. These are cast in the Far East and do not have the same high value as the 19th-century example shown here.
£3,000–5,000/ $4,500–7,500

LEAD

Although many lead ornaments were made in the 18th century the popularity of this material waned in the 19th century. As lead is such a soft material it begins to look old fairly rapidly because the weight of the material presses down on the body of the piece. For example, if an urn has a narrow foot it tends to collapse onto it. The vast majority of lead urns that are in existence today therefore date from the middle, or even the end, of the 20th century.

▲ **Pair of lead planters by the Bromsgrove Guild, early 20th century**
Although a little battered these would still fetch a good price.
£1,500–2,500/$2,250–3,750

◄ **Lead urn, possibly by the Bromsgrove Guild, late 19th century**
It is unusual to find a lead ornament that was produced in the 19th century. The quality of chiselling, the modelling, and the sheer presence of this piece all point to it being produced by the Guild. **£2,000–3,000/$3,000–4,500**

THE BROMSGROVE GUILD

The Bromsgrove Guild of Applied Arts was established in 1898 by Walter Gilbert when he took over an existing foundry in Bromsgrove, Worcestershire. It was first involved with decorative ironwork, but the business soon expanded into a great many other fields. By 1900 Gilbert had gone into partnership with a Mr McCandlish and had taken over further premises in the town, which housed bronze and lead foundries as well as wood- and stone-carving studios. By 1908 they had established an outlet in London and, as a result of their most famous commission (the iron and bronze gates outside Buckingham Palace), they were issued with a Royal Warrant appointing them metal workers to Edward VII – an honour repeated two years later under George V. Unlike the garden ornaments of many other contemporary English manufacturers, most of the Guild's figurative subjects were modelled in the popular styles of the day. In 1921 the Guild became a limited company, but by this date some of its members had left to start their own companies. However, it continued to produce a variety of quality garden ornaments for many years until it finally closed in 1966.

► **A lead planter, early 20th century**
This planter is moulded with putti and has ram's head ends – an unusual and appealing design. It is a sensible shape for a lead planter as the weight is evenly distributed and there is no narrow foot.
£400–600/$600–900

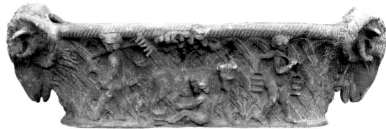

◄ ▲ **Two examples of 20th-century lead urns**
Each of these would have been part of a pair. The weight of the urn body on the narrow socle means that these urns have collapsed slightly, making them look much older than they really are.
£400–600/$600–900 (each pair)

► **A pair of Bromsgrove Guild lead planters, early 20th century**
The important thing to know about leadwork produced by the Bromsgrove Guild is that all the casting is of exceptional quality. Although prices for these urns are very high they should hold their value as they are rare and much sought after.
£5,000–8,000/$7,500–12,000

► Lead urn, late 20th century
This was probably made very late in the 20th century but it is a copy of a 16th-century design. Lead weathers so quickly that this could be mistaken as an early piece, but the patina reveals that it is fairly modern.
£250–350/$375–525

Modern leadwork is uniform in colour, as shown here, so attempts are often made to replicate an antique patina.

◄ Lead finial, late 20th century
This modern lead finial is impressive due to its immense size, but the quality of the decorative modelling is not in the same league as the modern urn pictured above.
£800–1,200/$1,200–1,800

CAST IRON

The Industrial Revolution, which occurred in the late 18th/early 19th centuries, saw the development of sand casting and efficient blast furnaces. This enabled metal ornament to be reproduced cheaply and well. Consequently a vast number of cast-iron urns and finials were manufactured, and a great many of these are still in existence today. The popularity of cast-iron garden ornament has meant that there are also many modern reproductions of antique originals on the market.

▶ **Heraldic finial, mid-19th century**
This is a rare cast-iron heraldic finial in the form of a stag's head. It would have been one of a pair of finials that were set either side of a gateway.
£1,500–2,500/ $2,250–3,750 (for one) or £4,000–6,000/ $6,000–9,000 (the pair)

THE BORGHESE & MEDICI URNS

The Borghese and Medici urns are perhaps the most well known, and most copied, of all antique marble originals. They were discovered in separate locations in Italy at the end of the 16th century. They are often presented as a pair, despite the fact that the Borghese vase has no handles and the lower section of each one is carved quite differently: the Borghese urn is lobed while the Medici urn is carved with acanthus and foliage. Both urns were copied in bronze for the Bassin de Latone gardens at Versailles, France.

▲ **Copy of the Medici urn in cast iron, 19th century**
This famous urn has been copied in a huge variety of materials. There has been much discussion about the origin of the classical frieze, but scholars have not been able to identify the subject matter. The original marble vase is on display in the Uffizi Gallery in Florence.
£800–1,200/$1,200–1,800

◄ **A pair of cast-iron urns by the Handyside Foundry,** *c.*1860
A pair of cast-iron urns by the Handyside Foundry, *c.*1860
The double lotus shape is peculiar to this foundry and is based on earlier Georgian designs. **£600–1,000/$900–1,500**

MODERN COPIES

These are often cast in the Far and Middle East, where labour is cheaper than it is in Europe. It is possible to obtain a modern copy of a 19th-century cast-iron urn for about a tenth of the price of an original. Of course there is a downside to this: modern copies are not of the same quality and therefore will not pass the test of time in the same way that a genuine Victorian casting does.

The many layers of paint have begun to obscure the crispness of this casting.

▲ ► Examples of Victorian cast-iron urns
These two pictures show part of the wide variety of Victorian cast-iron urns that are available today. Although there is some rust evident, the castings are on the whole still crisp. As a result of the presence of many modern copies the price of such originals has dropped slightly.
£150–1,200/$225–1,800 (each)

FOUNTAINS & WATER ORNAMENTS

Water is at the very heart of a garden – a life force that brings interest to the eye and tranquillity to the spirit. The inclusion of water in gardens evolved from the need to irrigate in dry areas. Both the Romans and the Greeks recognized the decorative potential of water features, but perhaps the greatest debt for the use of water in gardens is owed to the Muslims of the Middle Ages, who refined it to an art form.

The use of straight stretches of water in an existing landscape has been exceedingly effective in many of the great gardens of Europe. The spectacular Renaissance villas in Italy utilized the decorative force of water in abundance, but probably the most sumptuous use can be seen in the gardens of Versailles in France. The great canal at Hampton Court Palace, built by Cardinal Wolsey and renovated by Henry VIII for Anne Boleyn, is another example of this extravagant employment of water for decoration. It is said that Charles II then installed the water course in an attempt to emulate Versailles.

Formal gardens began to emerge in Britain at the end of the 15th century. The Tudors designed intricate knot gardens set around geometric pools, and water channels and ponds were centred with water spouts or fountains. These formal gardens were often uprooted in the 18th century, to be replaced with more naturally landscaped gardens. The fashion for great vistas, huge lakes, waterfalls, and temples, designed so that the eye could travel to the horizon from one "natural" feature to another, meant that a great many formal English gardens were lost.

Today we have all the advantages of modern design and technology, as well as being able to draw on designs of the past. Practically every time you turn on the television you can find a programme on garden design. There is usually someone showing you how to make a "water feature" out of various materials originally designed for another use. However, if you wish to install a fountain in your garden you will obtain a better effect if you utilize something designed for the purpose, such as the antique water ornaments available.

MARBLE

It is necessary to think carefully before installing a marble fountain in a cold climate. For example, whereas Istrian or Rosso Verona would adapt perfectly well to a northern European climate a white-marble fountain would be damaged. Most of such fountains found in Britain are produced in Italy, where the climate is more temperate. However, the late 20th century saw an increase in the production of marble ornament from the Far East. Such pieces obviously do not bear any of the signs of wear that you would expect to find on a 19th-century Italian original.

◄ A Rosso Verona wellhead, Italian, 17th century
This is an original 17th-century wellhead, but there are a great many late 19th-century and even 20th-century copies of this particular type. It can be used as a water feature or can be planted out with flowers.
17th-century: £10,000–15,000/$15,000–22,500
20th-century copy: £6,000–8,000/$9,000–12,000

▲ A white-marble fountain, Italian, late 19th century
This type of fountain is very popular today, but white marble is a difficult medium to use with water in a cold climate and would need to be protected during the winter months.
£3,000–5,000/$4,500–7,500

▲ A white-marble fountain, Italian, late 19th century
Another example of a traditional Italian fountain, this one has a carved baluster. Such an elegant design would do well in a courtyard garden or as the central feature on a lawn or terrace.
£6,000–10,000/$9,000–15,000

STONE & COMPOSITION STONE

If you are thinking of installing a fountain in a cold climate then stone or composition stone are probably the best options. Original, hand-carved stone fountains are scarce and expensive but composition stone can be bought at a relatively affordable price. One of the advantages of composition stone is that you can order it direct from the manufacturer. The parts of the fountain will be sold separately so that you can make up the exact design you want. Once the fountain has been set up and the water has been pouring over it for a year or so it will attain the desirable "weathered" look.

▲ **A carved stone gargoyle, French, 19th century**
This is an architectural feature, designed to be viewed from below. It could be adapted easily for a water feature in a garden, perhaps on a wall above a pool.
£800–1,200/$1,200–1,800

▲ **A carved Vicenza stone wellhead, Italian, late 20th century**
This is carved to resemble a typical 18th-century Italian wellhead, but the stiffness of the design marks it out as a 20th-century piece. As Vicenza stone is so soft the wellhead should weather quickly.
£4,000–6,000/$6,000–9,000

▲ **A composition-stone figural fountain, Bromsgrove Guild, early 20th century**
This shows the quality of design and the workmanship of pieces produced by the Bromsgrove Guild. The modelling is exact and the whole piece is very pleasing to the eye. This popular model can be found in lead as well as composition stone.
£4,000–6,000/$6,000–9,000

TERRACOTTA & STONEWARE

The interest in garden design at the end of the 19th and beginning of the 20th centuries meant that most of the well-known potteries produced some kind of water ornament. Some of these were so large and ornate that they would only be suitable for use in a park or a large country house, whereas others are more easily incorporated into a small garden. The terracotta or stoneware produced for this purpose was frostproof and, with a little care, can be allowed to remain *in situ* during an average winter.

COADE STONE

Coade stone is a fired clay aggregate that was developed by Mrs Eleanor Coade (1733–1821). Her aim was to produce an artificial stone that resembled carved stone in every respect. The Coade factory, situated in Lambeth, was founded in 1769 and produced its stonework to order. The early Coade pieces are marked Coade Lambeth. Later, John Sealy became a partner and pieces made after 1799 are marked Coade and Sealy.

Coade not only copied antique originals, such as the Medici and Borghese urns, but also modelled Classical subjects. The sculptor John Bacon was employed by Mrs Coade to produce classical sculpture. He began his association with Mrs Coade as an employee but, as his reputation increased, he became superintendent of the Coade Manufactory.

Coade stone has a unique formula that makes it impervious to frost and to the ravages of northern European weather. Because it is dry-cast and fired the detail is very crisp, and so it is possible to produce many elaborate pieces. Coade stone is a warm golden-beige colour, and has a slightly shiny surface, unlike terracotta, which has a matt surface and is therefore susceptible to damp. Twenty years ago you could pick up a piece of Coade stone for just a few pounds, but now its high value quite justly reflects the quality and importance of this material.

◀ **A fountain mask of a river god made in stone, Coade Lambeth, late 18th century**
Coade stone is the most valuable and sought after of all stoneware ornament.
£3,000–4,000/$4,500–6,000

▲ **A stoneware fountain, Doulton, early 20th century**
Stamped "Royal Doulton", this piece has a good, warm, golden-beige colour and is of a very manageable size.
£4,000–6,000/$6,000–9,000

▲ **Two figural birdbaths, Doulton, early 20th century**
Doulton produced a range of garden ornaments based on animals and birds. The base above left is designed to be placed underwater so that the pelican looks as if it is standing on the surface. **Pelican: £1,000–1,500/ $1,500–2,250. Cranes: £600–1,000/$900–1,500**

▶ **Stoneware fountain, Doulton, early 20th century**
Stamped "Doulton, Lambeth", this is a very attractive fountain. The scallop-shell detail in the design would fit in well with any water-based garden scheme. **£2,000–3,000/ $3,000–4,500**

DOULTON

Recognizing the demand for garden ornament in the early part of the 20th century, Henry Doulton began to make terracotta during the 1900s. To begin with the company produced female figures in a classical style, but as the century progressed Doulton garden ornaments reflected the varying enthusiasms of the time. The range was extended to include sundials, window boxes, and garden edging; many of these designs were produced in both red terracotta and stoneware. Brightly coloured majolica-glazed pieces were made between 1875 and 1910.

The company became Royal Doulton in 1902 and by this time it had a full range of garden ornament. After World War I the range began to reflect the smaller-scale, more intimate nature of both public and domestic horticulture. There were fewer fountains, and more birdbaths, garden gnomes, and animals.

The quality of the modelling on Doulton pieces is often quite exceptional.

AMERICAN WATER ORNAMENT

The use of zinc as a material for garden ornaments is very unusual in Britain, but it was used frequently by American manufacturers and designers. Both the Mott Foundry and the Fiske Foundry developed a range of garden ornaments cast in zinc, and some of their fountains are the most decorative to be found.

The American taste for naturalistic subjects meant that many of these fountains were decorated with birds or animals. Most of the fountains were of a relatively small scale, although there are some exceptions. Today you will pay a premium for any American piece as they are extremely popular.

FISKE FOUNDRY

Joseph Winn Fiske established an ornamental ironworks in New York in 1858. He enjoyed a prosperous existence and made all varieties of ornamental iron. Around 1899 his sons John W. Fiske and Joseph W. Fiske joined the firm. It was one of the first foundries to popularize the use of alloys and zinc for the figures in fountains. Unlike iron, these materials were not susceptible to rust. Not all Fiske's wares were marked.

◄ **A rare zinc fountain, Fiske Foundry, late 19th century**
The use of a water bird is typical of Fiske design. This is a particularly sought-after item because the bird is modelled in great detail, and because it is one of the rarer Fiske pieces. **£4,000–6,000/$6,000–9,000**

ZINC

Zinc has been used in garden ornamentation since the mid-19th century. German manufacturer Professor Kiss displayed a wide range of zinc sculptures at the Great Exhibition of 1851 to much acclaim, but it was the Americans who produced the majority of zinc garden ornaments. The advantages of the metal are that it is light, cheap, and corrosion-resistant. It has a silvery appearance, which dulls to grey when left outside. It is easy to confuse with spelter, which is a zinc alloy, but in financial and practical terms there is too little difference to worry about distinguishing them. Both metals can develop spots if left outside, and care should be taken to protect pieces by painting them as the metals may become brittle with age. The materials can also be confused with lead, but both are considerably lighter and more rigid.

▲ **Zinc egret fountain, American, *c*.1900**
This is a good example of American design, as it represents an American bird; it is a very popular piece. **£2,000–3,000/$3,000–4,500**

LEAD & BRONZE

Both lead and bronze have the advantage of not rusting when wet. Although some lead fountains and fountain figures were made in the 18th century, the vast majority of existing lead water features were produced in the 20th century. There are also many lead foundries producing reproductions today of earlier pieces. Bronze is an expensive material, so an antique bronze fountain will set you back a few thousand pounds/dollars. You are not likely to find a large fountain in bronze, but there are many fountain figures. Again, there are now reproductions, mostly cast in the Far East, but the quality of these reproductions is nowhere near that of a European 19th-century original.

▲ Georgian lead cistern, early 18th century
This piece has ownership initials and is dated 1734. There are a great many modern copies of 18th-century cisterns, but this is an original. You can tell this by the dark patination present, which lead acquires through age, as well as by the quality of workmanship, which was of a high level in the 18th century.
18th-century version: £3,000–5,000/$4,500–7,500
Modern copy: £1,500–2,000/$2,250–3,000

One of the allures of period leadwork is the wonderful patina that it develops.

LEAD CISTERNS

Original 17th- and 18th-century lead cisterns are much sought after but there are many modern copies. To check that you have found an original, see if the decoration is on all sides of the cistern – 18th-century cisterns were made to collect water from the gutters of a house so would not have been decorated on the back (quite often only the front was decorated). There should be the remains of a tap and, if the cistern is of any size, there should also be strengthening struts on the inside. Most modern copies are rather over-decorated and have spurious dates. A cistern is a difficult thing to move and so, once *in situ*, would probably have been kept with the house; therefore a genuine antique cistern should have a provenance.

▶ Georgian lead cistern, early 18th century
Smaller cisterns are often more sought after than large ones as they fit more easily into modern gardens. The patination and crispness of the panelling confirm this to be an early cistern.
£2,500–4,000/$3,750–6,000

MODERN LEAD

Lead is perhaps the most widely misunderstood material in garden design. Because it is heavy and soft it rapidly becomes battered and looks much older than it really is. Very little lead was produced in the 19th century – it was not decorative enough for the Victorians, who preferred bronze, cast iron, and marble. Most of the lead urns made to 18th-century designs that are still in evidence today have actually been made in the 20th, or even the 21st, century. There are several lead foundries in production today who make copies of "18th-century" vases and finials, and once they have been in your garden for 20 years or so it is easy to see why people assume them to be 18th-century originals. However, the 18th-century pieces would have been hand-chiselled once they came out of the mould and the decorative detail should still be sharp today. The colour of old lead is also dark and the surface very smooth, with a slight shine to it, while new lead is grey and flaky looking. Owing to the weight of the lead, any urn made with a narrow foot will have collapsed down onto its socle after a few years of service.

▲ **After Verrochio: a bronze fountain in the form of a cherub holding a fish, Italian, late 19th century**
The original of this design was made for a fountain in the garden of the Medici villa at Careggi (it is now in the Palazzo Vecchio in Florence). Verrochio, a Renaissance artist, was a pupil of Donatello and himself taught Leonardo da Vinci. This charming group is much copied and can be found in lead, cast iron, and composition stone.
£2,500–4,000/$3,750–6,000

◄ **Modern cistern set with a modern lead fountain, H. Crowther Ltd, 20th century**
Although the panelling is similar to that of an 18th-century cistern, this is quite the wrong shape for an original as it could not possibly have been set against a wall. However, it works very well, and would look good in the centre of a lawn or a formal garden.
£2,000–3,000/$3,000–4,500

CAST IRON

There's no getting away from the fact that cast iron will rust unless it is specially treated, but if it does receive this treatment then a cast-iron fountain can be very serviceable. The many cast-iron foundries in the 19th century that produced garden ornaments also produced fountains; these companies include Coalbrookdale, Handyside, and the Sun Foundry in Britain, and the Val D'Osne Foundry in France. If you decide on a cast-iron fountain you are going to be spoilt for choice.

HANDYSIDE

Andrew Handyside (1806–87) purchased the Britannia Iron Works on the bank of the River Derwent in Derby in 1848. According to the paper *The Art Journal*, by 1850 Handyside was producing "several ornamental vases many of which were remarkable for their classical purity of form and ornament", as well as at least one fountain. The following year, at The Great Exhibition, Handyside was awarded a medal for its exhibits, which included castings, reduced copies of the Medici urn, and portrait busts of various notables such as Shakespeare, Milton, and Wellington. The quality of casting was exceptional and the foundry went from strength to strength from that moment on. In 1873 the business became a limited company and in the following year it published a catalogue of its ornamental wares.

▲ **An impressive fountain, Handyside, 19th century**
The three tiers here sit above an ornate base. This design is not suitable for most gardens, and probably was designed originally for a park. The fountain is sectional, which means it would have been made up from various components in the Handyside catalogue.
£5,000–8,000/$7,500–12,000

◀ **A cast-iron fountain, Handyside, *c.*1860**
This small fountain would fit into most gardens and is of a type that is popular today.
£1,500–2,500/ $2,250–3,750

◄ A classic fountain, Handyside, c.1880
This type of fountain is very sought after, as it is appropriate for almost any garden design. The shallow bowl at the foot should be sunk into the ground.
£5,000–8,000/ $7,500–12,000

Old rust showing through the paint on a piece of 19th-century cast-iron ornament.

◄ A cast-iron fountain, French, 19th century
Dating to the end of the 19th century, this piece is stamped "A Chapee Le Mans". The rather municipal design of this fountain makes it suitable for a formal garden.
£2,000–3,000/$3,000–4,500

▲ A cast-iron fountain, Coalbrookdale, c.1870
This model is one of the most attractive Coalbrookdale models and is much sought after. Originally it would have been painted in naturalistic colours – the swans white, with the fountain perhaps green – but nowadays such items are often painted in one colour.
£2,000–3,000/$3,000–4,500

▲ A rare fountain, Sun Foundry, *c.*1880
This is a very decorative fountain and is typical of the work produced by the Sun Foundry. It is stamped "George Smith, Sun Foundry, Glasgow".
£3,000–5,000/$4,500–7,500

► A modern cast-iron fountain, 20th century
A popular model copying a 19th-century original, this is a good example of contemporary cast iron and has the advantage of a coat of zinc paint below the top layer, which prevents rusting.
£1,000–1,500/$1,500–2,250

CARE OF FOUNTAINS

Northern temperate climates place strains on all types of material left outside, through the sheer variety of conditions that are experienced. Fountains are in need of particular attention during the colder months of the year because, by definition, they involve the use of water. The danger comes from ice because when water freezes it expands so, just as you would lag the water pipes in your house to minimize the risk of bursting, a little care must be exercised on your fountain. The easiest course of action to lessen the likelihood of damage is to leave the fountain running throughout the year. If the cold weather lasts for a period of days then it is best either to drain the fountain or to fit a device that heats the water above freezing point.

SUNDIALS

O ne of the earliest ways developed by man to tell the time was by
following the passage of the sun through the skies. The sun can also
track the seasons, which enabled the development of a rough calendar.

The earliest references to sundials come from Babylonian and Egyptian
texts of the first millennium BC. Even though mechanical clocks were fairly
widespread in Europe by the 14th century, the sundial was only superseded
by the use of radio time-signals as recently as the 20th century.

As lives became more and more structured by time, with the rapid growth
of factories in the late 18th century as well as the development of the railway
in the 19th, clocks had to be checked for accuracy and more sophisticated
dials were developed as a result. "Dialling", as the manufacture of sundial
plates has been termed, became quite competitive, with mathematicians
calculating dials that could show all sorts of astronomical data.

The pedestals of sundials also took on increased significance, as
dials were placed in more prominent positions as a testament to their
importance. The pedestals followed architectural and furniture fashions.
The vast majority of sundial pedestals are of baluster form, the detailing
or material giving clues to their ages.

Once travel between Europe and North America became common most
garden ornament was imported, reproduced, and adopted by the Americans.
The sundial is no exception, and sundials dating to the 18th century made
by American instrument makers are in existence today. English-made dials
especially calibrated for the latitudes of America were also produced.

It is not unusual for dials to have become separated from their pedestals.
Sundials require as much of the sun's arc as possible to maximize their use
so they were normally sited in fairly exposed positions, and have suffered
accordingly. Well-preserved examples are therefore at a premium. The
intricacy or style of the pedestal will also influence the value. Age does
not necessarily increase value, but it does add to the piece's interest.

▲ **A Portland-stone sundial,** *c.*1830,
with a circular bronze plate dated 1722
It is good to find an early plate with such
a distinguishable date. The pedestal is also
unusual because it is strongly carved.
£1,000–2,500/$1,500–3,750

◄ **A sandstone
sundial pedestal,
late 18th century**
The swags of flowers
suspended from the lion
masks indicate that this
pedestal dates to the
18th century, as this was
a popular Georgian design.
The pedestal would need
a large sundial plate, but
the plates of the 18th
century were often very
large, so if a suitable one
were found this would
be a very impressive piece.
**£1,500–2,500/
$2,250–3,750**

▲ **A Portland-stone sundial pedestal,
late 18th century**
Most sundial pedestals are of this form – a
simple baluster with a circular or square top.
This one is generous, and nicely weathered.
£1,500–2,500/$2,250–3,750

TYPES OF DIAL

The number of different sorts of dial that have been developed
over the history of sundials is large and is a result of their long
and widespread use. However, the most commonly seen types
can be broken down into four main categories:

- Horizontal plates with upright gnomons – this is the oldest
  type of dial.

- Vertical plates, which are mounted on suitably aligned walls;
  these were first recorded in Roman times.

- Armillary spheres, which were used for astronomical
  information as well as for telling the time. These consist of
  metal rings placed centrally around a rod that is aligned with
  the Earth's axis, and were first mentioned in the Renaissance.

- Heliochronometers, which were the most recent sort of "dial"
  to be invented. These were the most accurate of all, and many
  were still in regular use during the 1930s (*see box on page 52*
  for further information).

Rarer examples of sundials are the Scottish multiple dials and
the pillar sundial, which again is typically Scottish although
known throughout Britain.

◀ **Plain granite baluster, mid-19th century**
This is probably the most satisfactory pedestal, owing to its simplicity of form. Even so, granite is comparatively cheap as it tends to be associated with municipal works. **£1,000–1,500/ $1,500–2,250**

◀ **Bronze heliochronometer, 20th century, on an 1880 pedestal**
This heliochronometer has been inscribed "Pilkington & Gibbs Ltd, Preston, England". As the pedestal is Victorian but the heliochronometer 20th century, it is evident that they have been put together some time during the last century.
£1,000–1,500/$1,500–2,250

Sandstone is soft so the surface erodes if left unprotected from frost.

◀ **A Victorian sandstone sundial, late 19th century**
This is a very typical example of Victorian design. The size of the pedestal suggests that it was intended for a park or large estate. The use of an octagonal base probably means that it was set at the junction of pathways.
£5,000–8,000/ $7,500–12,000

HELIOCHRONOMETERS

Heliochronometers were the most accurate of all dials as they compensated for the equation of time by first setting the month and day before a reading was taken. The first one was invented by George Gibbs in 1902; they were made subsequently by Pilkington and Gibbs and Negretti & Zambra. Before the invention of radio time-signals they were the best way to check mechanical clocks' accuracy, and were still being used in this way up until the 1930s. Many still work just as efficiently today.

▲ **A Negretti & Zambra heliochronometer, *c.*1920**
The maker's name together with the marble pedestal make this a desirable object.
£1,000–1,500/$1,500–2,250

▲ **A white-marble sundial, *c.*1900**
This baluster pedestal, carved with wrythen decoration, is based on a Georgian design. It is possible to obtain a similar style in composition stone at a much lower cost.
£1,200–1,800/$1,800–2,700

Such details add to the appeal of a piece.

◀ **Figural sundial pedestal with octagonal bronze plate, by Doulton**
The pedestal is flanked by four figures of children representing the seasons. Doulton made a variety of pedestals of this kind at the turn of the 19th and 20th centuries. It is made of terracotta, which gives it its warm pink colour.
£3,000–5,000/$4,500–7,500

▲ **A carved-stone wall sundial, *c.*1900**
The sundial is carved with the platitude "Time Flies". This kind of wall sundial was popular in Scotland. **£500–800/$750–1,200**

DATES & PLATITUDES

Sundials were usually made either by opticians, who in the 18th and 19th centuries also made scientific instruments, or by clockmakers, so the value of a dial often depends on the significance of a particular maker. As early dials were often quite complicated mathematical instruments the makers tended to sign and date the plates. Other information was inscribed on the dials – most commonly the latitude and longitude that the dial was designed for, as every location requires a subtly different calibration. When time across Britain was standardized in the mid-19th century dials had to be altered to tell London time. Platitudes such as "Tempus Fugit" and "Count Only the Sunny Hours" appeared towards the end of the 19th century, and are normally an indication that a dial is a 20th-century reproduction. A great many 20th-century dials carry false dates. Modern dials are mass-produced and therefore the name of the manufacturer, even if it is marked on the dial, makes no difference to the value.

▲ **Reproduction bronze sundial plate, probably by Pearson Page of Birmingham, 20th century**
This reproduction plate bears the date 1705 but was actually made at the beginning of the 20th century. It is a good example of the excessive decoration that was popular in the early 1900s (*see* box, page 54). **£40–50/$60–75**

◀ **A J.P. White Honiton-stone sundial, 20th century**
This is typical of the kind of piece produced by J.P. White, which manufactured and retailed a wide variety of garden ornament at the beginning of the 20th century. The armillary sphere makes this very attractive to a modern buyer as they are extremely popular. **£2,000–3,000/ $3,000–4,500**

FAKE SUNDIAL PLATES

An early sundial plate was a precise instrument calibrated for a particular location. Other than the maker's name, and maybe address, the information engraved onto a plate was functional, so a plate with frivolous information, such as a platitude, should immediately raise suspicion if it is being offered as an antique. The enormous surge in popularity of garden statuary in the late 19th and early 20th centuries prompted several companies to produce sundials and plates in the fashionable 18th-century styles. The most notable was Pearson Page of Birmingham, England. Most later ones are instantly recognizable, although they were made in the same way as the originals. None was engraved with the latitude it was designed for, as they were not specifically calibrated. Few were signed, but even if they are the quality is not as good.

The material a plate is made from can also offer clues. In the 18th century plates were rarely made from anything other than bronze or slate, so any lead plate can only be 20th-century, even though it may suggest an earlier date. Extremes in size can also be an indicator of age, as many of the later plates were much smaller.

Look at the underside of the plate if you can, as the gnomon on an old sundial will be a separate piece fitted to the plate with iron pins, and the pins should show oxidation (although gnomons may come adrift from their plates if the fixing pins disintegrate).

▶ **A circular slate sundial plate, early 20th century**
This is 36cm (14in) in diameter – such large sundial plates are sought after because they fit onto generous pedestals to make important centrepieces to gardens. The dial is signed "Edwin Monk" and has a decorative bronze gnomon.
£200–300/$300–450

◀ **A Portland-stone sundial, 20th century**
This unusual example shows the use of both stone and lead to make up a sundial, as the pedestal has been flanked by four lead putti. Such examples are difficult to find and are therefore worth a lot in today's market.
£1,500–2,500/$2,250–3,750

LEFCO

LEFCO stands for the Leeds Fireclay Company, which started operating at the end of the 19th century and is still in existence today. Its distinctive pale-buff stoneware, which has an almost glazed finish, was once cheap to buy but has recently become popular. It is plentiful and all pieces are well stamped.

◄ **A Liberty & Co. terracotta sundial, early 20th century**
This was probably made by the Potters Art Guild. The design is simple but effective, and reflects the taste for slightly "mystic" designs – this one has been moulded with the rays of the sun.
£2,000–3,000/$3,000–4,500

▼ **Armillary sphere set on an earlier pedestal, late 20th century**
Although the sphere is modern the use of a Victorian pedestal increases the value.
£1,000–1,500/$1,500–2,250

▲ **A Compton Pottery sundial, early 20th century**
Illustrated in the 1908 catalogue of the Potters Art Guild, this sundial is referred to as "The Priory Pedestal". Compton Pottery pieces are very collectable, and this is a particularly attractive example of the Guild's work.
£2,500–4,000/ $3,750–6,000

▲ **A carved Vicenza-stone sundial, late 20th century**
This is a modern piece, carved during the 1990s but reflecting an earlier style. Vicenza stone weathers quickly so will soon look much older than it really is.
£3,000–5,000/$4,500–7,500

GARDEN FURNITURE

The inclusion of furniture in garden design is a relatively modern idea; indeed gardening as a leisure activity was something more or less unheard of before the beginning of the 20th century. It was not until after World War I, when it became difficult to find gardeners, that the middle classes started to tend their gardens themselves.

Before the 18th century the only kind of seating to be used outdoors would have been marble, plain stone, or wooden benches. Of course if a wooden bench had been left outside for 300 years or so it would have rotted and been thrown away, so any 16th- and 17th-century garden seating surviving today is of carved stone or marble. We have the Romans to thank for the introduction of marble benches – they made them in Italy and used them in their bath houses there.

The wrought-iron garden seats of the 18th century were not mass-produced but were made on a "one-off" basis by estate blacksmiths. The strapwork of the benches was of reeded wrought iron and the benches were simple in design, rather in the style of a wooden bench. These benches had little pad feet that turned at right angles to the legs to prevent the slender iron supports from sinking into the ground.

It was not until the great iron foundries of the 19th century began to produce garden furniture that it became widely available to the middle classes. The big advantage of cast-iron furniture was that it could be mass produced relatively cheaply. The Coalbrookdale Company of Ironbridge, Shropshire began by making domestic ironwork such as gutters and drainpipes, as well as large engineered pieces, but began to develop a range of garden furniture in the middle of the 19th century. This consisted mainly of seats but also included some tables and plant stands.

If you invest in antique garden furniture it should increase in value – and it has already stood the test of time. It was made to last and, as long as it is properly treated, it will serve you well for a lifetime.

MARBLE, STONE, & STONEWARE

Garden furniture did not appear in the majority of English gardens until well into the 19th century. Before that time only the very rich had gardens used simply for pleasure. Plain stone seating has been around since Roman times, and marble seats were imported from Italy when the English upper classes started to travel on the Continent. The use of terracotta or stoneware for garden seating is relatively rare, but the existing examples show the skill of the potters. Both terracotta and stone have the advantage of taking warmth from the sun, which is of great benefit in a colder climate.

▲ A white-marble seat, Italian, late 19th century
This is an impressive seat – such items are common in Italy but not so usual in England as the climate is unkind to marble. The material is damaged by sub-zero temperatures and will not keep its pristine whiteness unless covered up or kept inside during the winter. **£6,000–10,000/$9,000–15,000**

▼ A Bath-stone seat, 19th century
This is much more decorative than the Portland seat below as it is an example of Victorian Gothic design. The lion ends may well have been carved as a detail from a coat-of-arms, and seats of this kind are rare and therefore highly collectable. **£4,000–6,000/$6,000–9,000**

▲ A plain Portland-stone seat, c.1830
The seat is slightly weathered but as Portland stone is so durable not much erosion has occurred. The seat is fairly small, 127cm (50in) wide – just big enough to accommodate a Victorian lady in a hooped skirt. **£1,500–2,500/$2,250–3,750**

◄ A stone stool, French, 19th century
This is a very unusual piece, and has been included here mainly because it is so quirky and amusing. There seems to be no reason for the addition of the mask faces above the huge paw feet, and the tassels also seem to be pure decorative embellishment. **£1,500–2,000/$2,250–3,000**

◄ **A pair of stone benches,
late 18th/early 19th century**
These are both examples of the most
common form of stone seating from the
18th and early 19th centuries. Modern
copies of this kind of seat are prolific
but the originals still attract high prices.
£5,000–8,000/$7,500–12,000

► **A pair of composition-stone
benches, 20th century**
As can be seen, these pieces look very much
like the carved stone benches in the photograph
above, but they are cast in a mould and are
much cheaper to buy. They are weathered,
which is the preferred look, but you can
buy them new at a much lower price and
then weather them yourself. If you apply the
right mixture they will attain this weathered
look in a few years. There are commercial
"weathering" products available but most
dealers will have their own special mixture
that they prefer to use.
£500–800/$750–1,200

◄ **A Georgian-style,
carved Bath-stone seat,
20th century**
This seat was probably
made at the beginning
of the 20th century, as a
copy of a Georgian design.
However, the workmanship
and style are such that it
is very difficult to date
it accurately.
**£2,500–4,000/
$3,750–6,000**

▲ **A rare Charlottenburg stoneware seat,
German, late 19th century**
This seat was obviously designed for use in a park or grand estate
and would not fit very happily into a small garden. However, the
exuberance of the design and the crispness of the moulding make
it a very attractive piece. **£3,000–5,000/$4,500–7,500**

▲ **A pair of Doulton stoneware seat ends, c.1900**
These are rare pieces as Doulton did not produce many items
on this scale. Once fitted with wooden slats this seat would
be a very handsome addition to a garden, and, owing to its
rarity, it should continue to increase in value.
£1,500–2,500/$2,250–3,750

▲ **A carved Vicenza-stone seat, late 20th century**
These elaborate seats are very popular today and are readily
available. There is still a Vicenza workshop in production and
pieces can be hand-carved to order. The swan ends on this
particular seat make it very desirable.
£1,500–2,500/$2,250–3,750

WROUGHT IRON

Before the onset of the Industrial Revolution if people wanted iron garden furniture they had to ask their local blacksmith to make it for them. Each piece would therefore have been unique and, unless the same blacksmith made a pair of seats or chairs, it is unlikely that there would be an exact copy anywhere else. In the 18th century wrought iron tended to be reeded, and it was only in later years that the slats were made of slightly rounded, smooth wrought iron.

▲ A pair of Regency reeded wrought-iron chairs, early 19th century
These are typical of the kind of strapwork design that was popular in the late 18th and early 19th centuries. It is more common to see benches rather than chairs so these examples would attract a high price. It is possible to obtain similar modern examples, but the strapwork would not be reeded. **£2,000–3,000/$3,000–4,500**

▲ A Victorian wirework seat, late 19th century
This is a pretty seat but not substantial, as it would have been made purely for decoration. Such seats are cheaper to buy today than they were ten years ago: when wirework prices rocketed in the early 1990s much modern wirework came onto the market, reducing the value of originals. **£400–600/$600–900**

► A reeded wrought-iron games seat, early 20th century
The wheels on the back of this seat meant that it could be manoeuvred around the garden so that its users could watch people playing croquet on the lawns. The footrest enabled ladies in long dresses to keep their skirts out of the mud. **£1,500–2,500/$2,250–3,750**

► **A Regency-style strap-iron tree seat, mid-19th century**
This seat was made in two halves so that it could be placed around a tree. Seats of this kind are very sought after, but it is also possible to purchase modern copies more cheaply.
£1,800–2,500/$2,700–3,750

◄ **Wrought-iron furniture, French, from the late 19th and early 20th centuries**
These seats each have a brass plaque at their centre that has "ARRAS" written on it. The seats are comfortable as well as attractive, and were originally used as park furniture in France. They are becoming more available throughout England, and their popularity means that they can attract high prices.
£2,500–3,000/$3,750–4,500 (the set)

► **Regency, reeded wrought-iron seat, early 19th century**
This has all the hallmarks of a Regency seat: the reeded struts, the pad feet, and the arabesques at the back. Originals such as this are scarce, and therefore valuable, but there are many modern reproductions available that will give you the same "look" at far less cost.
£1,500–2,500/$2,250–3,750

CAST IRON

The Coalbrookdale Iron Foundry, based at Ironbridge in Shropshire, is probably the best-known English foundry. Recognised today for the fact that it still produces the Aga cooker – that mainstay of middle-class life – Coalbrookdale developed a vast range of garden ornament and furniture in the 19th century. However, other foundries such as Carron and Falkirk, which originally specialized in domestic ironwork, also produced seats, and there were many other smaller foundries fulfilling the huge market for garden furniture that arose at the turn of the 19th and 20th centuries.

◀ **The Convolvulus seat, 1860**
This is the earliest recorded Coalbrookdale design. The official registered design dates from the early 19th century and is of a panel pierced with convolvulus flowers. This seat is made of pierced iron, which makes the whole piece extremely heavy – it looks lighter than it actually is.
£1,200–1,800/$1,800–2,700

▶ **The Nasturtium, *c*.1870**
This design (Registration No. 195629) was the second most common Coalbrookdale design. There were two sizes of seat, one 137.5cm (55in) and the other 183cm (73in) wide. There are also chairs made in this pattern. The seats are usually wooden but the front seat rail is iron and is sometimes cast with the company's name, "C.B. Dale Co.". Painting the seat in naturalistic colours, with the leaves green and the flowers yellow, is a modern addition. Coalbrookdale never decorated its seats in this way – they were always painted in one colour with a matt finish.
£2,500–4,000/$3,750–6,000

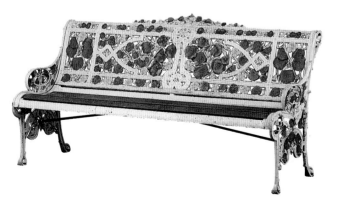

COALBROOKDALE

The Coalbrookdale Foundry was established in 1709 by Abraham Darby and was run by successive members of the Darby family throughout most of the 18th century. When the foundry started it confined its products to domestic wares and engineering castings, and produced the first iron rails in 1769. The famous Iron Bridge was made later, in 1799.

At the beginning of the 19th century the emerging affluence of the middle classes made it feasible for the company to produce a range of garden furniture and ornament in cast iron. The foundry made a vast number of seats, plant stands, urns, and fountains, as well as gates and railings. Its seats were very well cast and of sound construction – so much so that many of them are still in use today, although in most cases the wooden seat slats have been replaced.

The Coalbrookdale designs can be recognized by the fact that most of them are based on natural foliage. Hence the Fern and Blackberry seat, the Lily of the Valley, the Nasturtium, and a great many more – too many to list here but illustrated throughout this section of the book. The designs were practical as well as ornamental and were immediately popular. Leading sculptors, such as John Bell and Christopher Dresser, were commissioned to produce unique designs, and overall the company had a reputation for excellence. In 1851 Coalbrookdale exhibited a selection of its castings at the Great Exhibition and received a council medal. In 1875 the foundry published a huge illustrated catalogue comprising 12 sections of which Section III, "Garden and Park Embellishments", covers over 100 pages and provides a good insight into the Coalbrookdale range of garden ornament.

◄ **The Water Plant seat,** *c.*1870
Rather Art Deco in design, this seat (Registration No. 202162) has holes in the arms in order to accommodate a canopy. Victorian ladies were anxious not to get the sun on their faces, as a "healthy tan" gave the impression that one was not a lady of leisure but had to work in the garden.
£1,800–2,500/ $2,700–3,750

KITE MARKS

During the mid-19th century there was a system for registering patent designs referred to as "Kite Marks" – each one was a diamond shape, marked with letters and numbers in each corner. These marks help the collector to identify the date of registration, as well as the maker or retailer.

From 1842 to 1867 kite marks were arranged as follows: at the top is the year letter; left, the month letter; right, the day number; and at the bottom, the parcel number. From 1868 to 1883 the year letter moved to the right, the parcel number to the left, the day number to the top, and the month letter to the bottom. (A Registered Number was used after 1883.) The code letters were as follows:

1842–67		1868–83	
Years	Months	Years	Months
1842–X	Jan–C	1868–X	Jan–C
1843–H	Feb–G	1869–H	Feb–G
1844–C	Mar–W	1870–C	Mar–W
1845–A	Apr–H	1871–A	Apr–H
1846–I	May–E	1872–I	May–E
1847–F	Jun–M	1873–F	Jun–M
1848–U	Jul–I	1874–U	Jul–I
1849–S	Aug–R	1875–S	Aug–R
1850–V	Sept–D	1876–V	Sept–D
1851–P	Oct–B	1877–P	Oct–B
1852–D	Nov–K	1878–D	Nov–K
1853–Y	Dec–A	1879–Y	Dec–A
1854–J		1880–J	
1855–E		1881–E	
1856–L		1882–L	
1857–K *		1883–K	
1858–B			
1859–M			
1860–Z *			
1861–R			
1862–O			
1863–G			
1864–N	* R may be found as		
1865–W	the month mark for		
1866–Q	1st–9th Sept 1857,		
1867–T	and K for Dec 1860.		

1842–67

Year / Month / III Class / A / R^D / Day (25) / Parcel Nº (1)

1868–83

Parcel / III Class / 6 Day / R^D / Year / Month

▲ **Unnamed seat**
This seat is not named in Coalbrookdale's catalogue, but its registration number is 2104751. It was also produced as a double-sided seat – the back section formed the middle of two slatted seats – for parks and public gardens. This design is widely reproduced today, so if you are looking for an original seat you need to be wary.
£1,800–2,500/$2,700–3,750

▲ **The Horse Chestnut seat, *c.*1870**
This is a an attractive seat (Registration No. 17568), and is highly sought after today. It can be found in two sizes, as well as made up as a single chair.
£2,000–3,000/$3,000–4,500

◄ Eastern-influenced design, *c.*1870
Again this seat is registered (No. 90929) without the design having a name, but it seems to have a strong Eastern influence and was probably designed for export to the British living in India. It too is a design much reproduced today.
£1,500–2,500/$2,250–3,750

► Serpent and Grape design, *c.*1870
This early design (Pattern No. 9) is much copied today, especially in aluminium.
£800–1,200/$1,200–1,800

▲ The Gothic pattern, *c.*1870
This is a very attractive design (Pattern No. 22), and is also widely copied today. There are a great many made in aluminium as well as cast iron so be wary if you are looking for a 19th-century cast-iron original.
£2,500–4,000/$3,750–6,000 (the set)

MODERN COPIES

It is now possible to obtain modern copies of some of the most popular Coalbrookdale designs, as well as to find composition-stone copies of stone seats. The Coalbrookdale copies are made in cast iron and aluminium, and are less expensive to buy than originals; as a result they will not increase in value. Composition stone can be treated with various weathering agents so that in a few years it will look like weathered stone but, again, it will not increase in value in the same way that antique stone will.

▶ **Oval pattern,** *c.*1870
Another pattern with no official name, but the back is comprised of a run of oval paterae – fairly plain but a pleasing design. It is not as popular as some of the floral patterns and is therefore cheaper to buy on the present market.
**£2,000–3,000/
$3,000–4,500**

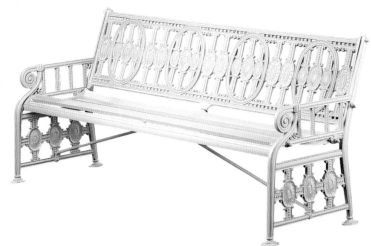

◀ **The Medieval pattern,** *c.*1870
This is a rare pattern (Registration No. 240809) and is therefore difficult to obtain. The casting at the back is quite flat, making the seat comfortable to sit on, and the whole design has a restrained elegance.
**£3,000–5,000/
$4,500–7,500**

▶ **The Osmundia Fern seat,** *c.*1870
This is another rare pattern (Registration No. 273254), but it is rather complicated and heavy looking and therefore is not as popular as some of the more common designs. This is reflected in its relatively modest value.
**£2,500–4,000/
$3,750–6,000**

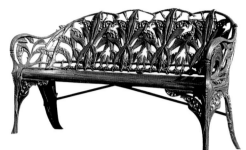

▲ **The Lily Of The Valley,** *c.*1870
This design (Registration No. 171578) was very popular, and there are many such seats still in use today.
£2,500–4,000/$3,750–6,000

VALUES OF CAST-IRON SEATS

Cast-iron seats, once they have been rust-proofed and painted, can be left outside in the winter and antique pieces should increase in value as the years go by. For example, a good Coalbrookdale Fern and Blackberry seat, which would have reached £250/$375 at auction in 1986, now makes around £2,000/$3,000. Some of the rarer patterns, such as the Passion Flower, can make huge amounts of money; one was sold to an American buyer in 1999 for £23,000/$34,500.

▲ **The Passion Flower seat,** *c.*1870
This is the most coveted pattern of all because it has everything: it is rare, very pretty, and smaller and lighter than most Coalbrookdale patterns. This design is particularly popular in the American market and can fetch very high prices (*see* box, left).
£6,000–10,000/$9,000–15,000

▲ **The Oak and Ivy,** *c.*1870
This is an example of the Victorian love of excessive decoration. The seat (Registration No. 119253) is rather clumsy, and very heavy to move around the garden, but it is also one of the designs that is copied a great deal today.
£3,000–5,000/$4,500–7,500

▲ **The Fern and Blackberry,** *c.*1870
This is the most common, and perhaps the most effective, Coalbrookdale design (Registration No. 941548). Although it is copied today it is not reproduced exactly, so it is fairly easy to distinguish originals from fakes (*see* box, opposite).
£800–1,200/$1,200–1,800

▶ **Edward Bawden design,
early 20th century**

Edward Bawden (1903–89) was a painter, illustrator, and graphic designer. The design for this seat (based on a spider's web) moves away from the flowers and foliage favoured by Victorian manufacturers and reflects a strong Art Deco influence. The seat is of interest but is not especially popular within the modern market.

£1,500–2,500/$2,250–3,750

COALBROOKDALE COPIES AND FAKES

The increasing popularity and value of 19th-century cast-iron seats have also meant an increase in the amount of copies and fakes on the market. There is nothing wrong with a copy; Coalbrookdale is still producing copies of some of its most popular patterns in cast iron, and in the mid-20th century produced a range in aluminium. These are cheaper to buy than the originals and are not intended to deceive as they are sold as "copies". A fake is another thing. To prevent yourself from being deceived into buying one, a few things to look out for are detailed below.

You can tell if a piece is cast iron or aluminium by putting a magnet onto it – a magnet will not stick to aluminium. Look at the nuts: they should be domed, made of bronze, and hand-cut; there should be no modern screw-heads. Then look at the casting – it should be crisp and of good quality. The piece should also be very heavy. It takes two people to lift a Coalbrookdale Fern and Blackberry seat – it is difficult even to lift one end on your own.

Now look at areas of rust. If a cast-iron seat has been outside for 150 years or more there will be some rust in the crevices where rainwater would lie, but it will not be an all-over rusting.

As you would take care if buying a used car for a few thousand pounds/dollars, so also take care when you buy antique cast-iron furniture. The main thing to remember is that Coalbrookdale and other 19th-century foundries were renowned for the quality of the goods they produced, so you should not find sloppy castings.

If you buy a piece at auction it is guaranteed to be what is described in the catalogue. Therefore, if you find that you have purchased a copy that was catalogued as an original, you can go back to the auctioneer and have your money refunded.

If you are buying from a shop go to a reputable dealer who will be happy to give you the provenance of the piece you are buying. It is probably best to resist the temptation of the car boot (garage) sale, where there is no proof of provenance and no comeback if the piece disappoints upon further inspection.

▲ **Four Seasons seat by Morgan, McCaulay & Wade of Rotherham, late 19th century**
This rare seat is very decorative. Each oval back section has been cast with flowers that relate to the different seasons.
£2,500–4,000/$3,750–6,000

▲ **Cast-iron bench by the Carron Foundry, mid-19th century**
The original signed drawing for this seat in the Carron Foundry catalogue is numbered 34358. Both the Carron and the Falkirk foundries were located on the Firth of Forth on the east coast of Scotland, but they had warehousing and retailing premises close to each other in Upper Thames Street, London, to which iron goods were transported along the River Thames.
£1,500–2,500/$2,250–3,750

▲ **A cast-iron seat by the Val d'Osne Foundry, French, c.1860**
This seat is attractive and fits in well with modern designs; however, it would not be very comfortable to sit on.
£1,000–1,500/$1,500–2,250

AMERICAN SEATS

The market for cast-iron garden furniture was not restricted to the UK – once the American public saw the variety of designs available in Britain they wanted similar pieces, but from an American manufacturer. Many US cast-iron foundries met this demand, with some patterns closely following the English originals while others were unique to the USA. All these seats are beginning to attract high prices because there is a strong American market for garden items that have been made in the USA.

◀ A rare J.L. Mott & Co. laurel-pattern seat, late 19th century
A similar seat is illustrated in the J.L. Mott Iron Works catalogue of 1889, plate 35. This is an adaptation of the laurel pattern that was made by the Coalbrookdale Company a few years earlier, although the design of the seat is slightly different. This seat has the maker's stamp on it, which adds to its value.
£5,000–8,000/$7,500–12,000

MOTT FOUNDRY

J.L. Mott & Co. started out as the Mott Iron Works stove business on Water Street, New York. Jordan L. Mott was the very wealthy principal partner who obtained an 1847 patent for a cast-iron revolving "opera chair". The business was worth approximately one million dollars in 1870. Between 1875 and 1878 Mott had a showroom at 549 Sixth Avenue, and by 1882 another had opened at 1255 Broadway.

▲ Cast-iron latticed seat, late 19th century
This design was produced by John F. Riley, a foundry based in Charleston, South Carolina.
£2,000–3,000/$3,000–4,500

AMERICAN COPIES

Many of the designs produced by Coalbrookdale in the mid-19th century were copied or amended by designers in the USA. The seats shown in this section are all similar to Coalbrookdale designs, although it is not certain who was copying whom – it is possible that the designers at Coalbrookdale copied from the American foundries. Owing to the interest in the USA in garden antiques, especially pieces designed and made in the States, such seats attract high prices. Interestingly, at the end of the Civil War the USA had an over-abundance of iron foundries, several of which diversified to produce garden ornaments.

▲ Fern seat, probably made by J.W. Fiske, late 19th century
This seat is pierced with geometric patterns. It has similarities with the Coalbrookdale Fern and Blackberry seat, but is more geometric and the pierced seat is typically American (pierced cast iron was favoured over wood probably owing to the often warmer climate). **£1,000–1,500/ $1,500–2,250**

► Passion Flower seat, late 19th century
This is very similar to the Coalbrookdale Passion Flower seat on page 68, but the piercing is slightly different in design.
£5,000–8,000/ $7,500–12,000

PUB TABLES

Pub tables are so-named because they originated in English public houses. The wooden furniture in inns and public houses was replaced with cast iron once it became available in the 19th century because it was cheap and could be cast in intricate designs. Such tables became so common that when pubs were remodelled the tables were often replaced. With so many on the market they are inexpensive, and also practical – being heavy they cannot be blown over or tipped up.

▲ Two cast-iron, Britannia-pattern "pub" tables, Gaskell and Chambers, late 19th century
Such tables were produced by many manufacturers, and there is a variety of patterns available. Sometimes the tops are pierced iron; others are wooden. The abundance of these tables means that they are relatively cheap to buy.
£80–120/$120–180 (each)

◄ Pierced iron-topped table, *c*.1880
This is more decorative than the vast majority of pub tables, and also a little smaller in diameter. The pierced top of this design is decorated with geometric patterns. The Falkirk Foundry produced a similar table with the top cast with the signs of the zodiac. Tables that have cast-iron tops are more expensive to buy than the smaller examples with wooden or marble tops.
£250–350/$375–525

▼ **Iron-ended tables, probably by Gaskell and Chambers, late 19th century**
These two tables are each made up from cast-iron ends with wooden tops that were
added quite recently. Tables of this kind are relatively cheap to buy, and are often made
up from the trestle supports of old sewing machines.
£300–500/$450–750 (each)

This is a detail of the cast-
iron pub table shown above
left. The cast includes a
portrait mask of the
cricketer W.G. Grace.

PUB TABLE DESIGNS

Pub tables were manufactured by a
great many foundries, in particular
Gaskill and Chambers, Lorn and
Howarth, and the Bicklam company,
which is an acronym of Bennets Iron
Foundry Co. Ltd, Hyde Road, Ardwick,
Manchester. There are many different
designs but by far the most common is
the Britannia pattern – a mask of the
face of Britannia on the shoulder of
each cabriole leg, and the legs joined
by a circular pierced iron stretcher
(*see* page 73). There was also a design
produced for Queen Victoria's Jubilee
featuring a mask of the Queen.

When they were first produced
pub tables would have had either
mahogany or marble tops, but it is
rare to find one with the original top.
If you do find a pub table with its
marble top it will have more value
than one with a replaced top, even
if the replacement is of finer quality
than the original.

The intricate, cast-iron frames of
such tables do not look out of place
in an indoor setting, and there are
many plainer tables that, with a bit
of paint and new tops, would work
very well in a garden location.

WOODEN FURNITURE

Although wooden garden furniture was widely used in the 18th and 19th centuries very little of it has survived, so most of what is seen today was made from the 1930s up to the present day. There are some ingenious designs among these – some incorporating boxes to keep garden games, others with flip backs so the user can face in either direction. Most of the designs that were popular in the 1930s and '40s have been reproduced, so you can obtain a new version of these quite easily.

▲ A teak Lutyens-style seat, 20th century
This is a very popular item, based on the kind of seat used by Edwin Lutyens in his garden designs. Look for a substantial seat and make sure that the lower stretchers are sound.
£800–1,200/$1,200–1,800

▲ A J.P. White wooden seat, early 20th century
J.P. White made a wide variety of wooden garden furniture, and the company's catalogue illustrates over 30 designs for seats. The quality of workmanship makes this a desirable item and so it will hold its value. **£800–1,200/$1,200–1,800**

◄ Steamer chair, *c*.1925–50
This is one of a pair of teak folding seats made from ships' timbers. This type of furniture was produced by shipbrokers, and this particular example has a maker's label on it: "Shipbreaking Co. Ltd Manufacturers, Millbank, London SW1". The addition of the maker's label adds slightly to the value, but if the label were to read that the timbers came from an historically important ship this would greatly increase its worth.
£200–300/$300–450

SCULPTURE

It is fortunate that the popularity of garden design and the growing understanding of the use of statues within it make it possible to find almost anything we could desire in the way of statuary for the garden. You want a Venus dipping her toe into your pond? You want a satyr playing the pipes in your shrubbery? You want cherubs? You want a set of the Four Seasons? You want an Italian garden set out with copies of famous antique statues? It is very easy to source all these pieces, at surprisingly low prices.

Once the English upper classes began to travel abroad they became enamoured of the many antique statues on display in Europe, especially the vast number of ornaments to be seen in Italy, and wished to have something similar in their estates in England. There was a flourishing business in Italy carving reproductions of the famous originals, so that by the beginning of the 18th century white-marble copies of most of the great antique statues to be found in France and Italy could be seen in English country gardens. Once the copies were in England they began to be copied in turn, and the process also developed in North America. In the 19th century there were large workshops in Italy where artists carved copies of antique pieces almost on a production line. If people had the financial means they could order statues to be copied and have them sent to their own estates.

In the 18th and 19th centuries statuary was hand-carved, whereas most of the copies seen today are made in moulds. In the case of marble statues the marble is ground down, mixed with resin as a wet mix, and then cast in the same way that cement can be cast. These do not have the quality of hand-carved pieces but from a distance have the look of originals. However, there is always an exception and, in this case, it is the quantity of carved marble statuary being produced in the Far East, particularly in China, and the Vicenza-stone carvings still being produced near Venice today.

Eyes are always drawn to a figure in a landscape, and there is a cast of hundreds to choose from to be the focal point of your own garden.

MARBLE

As mentioned previously, marble needs care in a cool climate, but nevertheless it is the most beautiful material to be used for sculpture. Most of the antique originals of famous statues were carved in marble, and you only have to look at a good marble carving to realize the instant appeal of this medium. It takes sharp detail better than any other type of stone and is so universally regarded that even damaged or weathered pieces are still desirable and sell for a premium.

▲ **A pair of white-marble lions after Canova, Italian, late 18th century**
These would be wonderful at the top of a flight of steps. They are very well carved, probably by one of the many Italian sculptors producing works for export at the turn of the 18th and 19th centuries.
£10,000–15,000/$15,000–22,500 (the pair)

▶ **A white-marble figure of Mercury, Italian, late 18th/early 19th century**
This is a good example of the statuary produced in Italy for the English market. The employment of the fig leaf is a good clue to the statue having been produced for more prudish buyers.
£8,000–12,000/$12,000–18,000

COMPOSITION MARBLE

Over the last 20 years or so composition marble has appeared. It mimics the natural stone and is made by crushing marble and bonding it together with cement or a resin. It can be very hard to tell the difference, but a composition piece is made by casting rather than carving so look out on an original for undercutting or sharp edges that are hard to produce in a mould. However, such marks are no guarantee as the better composition pieces are finished by hand-carving, so always buy from a reputable source. The sophistication of copies is such that even veining can be accurately recreated.

The Victorians thought nude statues indecent, and many figures originally carved as nudes were augmented by a fig leaf or a drape.

The surface condition affects the value of a piece. If this bust was in perfect condition it would be worth at least twice as much.

▶ **A white-marble portrait bust, French, late 19th century**
This was probably intended for someone's library but it has been left outside and the marble has abraded. Marble in this condition cannot be restored to its original surface and therefore such portrait busts are relatively affordable to buy today. **£1,000–1,500/$1,500–2,250**

▲ **A white-marble figure of a faun playing the cymbals, 18th century**
Although this figure is seated it is obviously based on the classical figure of the dancing faun (see page 92). **£6,000–10,000/$9,000–15,000**

◀ **A white-marble fairy, late 19th century**
An example of the Victorian taste, this is likely to have come from a graveyard where it would have been used as a memorial to a child. **£3,000–5,000/ $4,500–7,500**

▶ **Group of bacchantes, Prosper D'Epinay, late 19th century**
The sculptor of this figure is not well known, and the group is only 70cm (28in) in height, so this piece is quite affordable, especially as it is slightly damaged. **£1,000–1,500/$1,500–2,250**

STONE

Until the 20th century, when a great many composition materials and resins were used for garden statuary, figures in the garden tended to be carved in stone. Marble was expensive, and only the wealthy could afford it, whereas stone was not only readily available but was also more suited to the northern European climate. There is a huge variety of stones that have been used for garden ornament; all will weather in different ways and such weathering should be appreciated rather than cleaned off.

▲ A gritstone figure of a putto, early 18th century
This was probably produced in the Low Countries. Gritstone is incredibly difficult to carve, owing to its density; it is almost a granite, but it has the advantage that it does not erode and this figure looks as crisp today as it would have done when it was first produced.
£3,000–5,000/$4,500–7,500

The weathering of the carving is evident, but this does not affect the value as weathered stone is popular.

◀ ▲ A pair of carved Portland-stone putti, 19th century
Representing Spring and Autumn, these figures are 60cm (24in) in height. They are nicely weathered but still retain a good amount of detail.
£2,500–4,000/ $3,750–6,000 (the pair)

VICENZA STONE

Vicenza stone was one of the most popular stones used in the manufacture of garden statuary during the 20th century. The term describes a group of soft limestones found around the town of Vicenza, Italy. In northern temperate climates it looks old very quickly, as owing to its porous nature mosses and lichens grow fast to produce the desired "antique" look. In warmer, drier climes the stone lasts for a long time, and there are still pieces in good condition from the 16th century. In harsher climates the shelf-life of fine detail is shorter and so care should be taken to protect pieces in wet and cold weather.

The Scarmozzi and Palladio School in Vicenza was established in 1500 to decorate villas in the area, and it continued until c.1800, when stone was replaced by marble (although the workshops continued). In 1930 Rossato Giovanni, its director, began exporting from many stone workshops in the area, and Vicenza carvings are still being produced today. There are two main types of Vicenza stone: San Gottardo, Colli Berici – a fine-grained white-to-yellow stone, weathering to grey, and rich in fossil – and Pietra Gialla or Dorato, San Germano – a yellow stone with dark veins and fossil inclusions.

◄ **Stone dog, 19th century**
The English like their dogs and this is a great example of the popular sculpture of the day. It is likely that the dog is carved as a portrait of a favourite pet, as it has what may be a characteristically quizzical expression. It is possible to obtain composition stone models of seated dogs, but this hand-carved example has a naive charm that you do not find in mass-produced pieces. **£4,000–6,000/$6,000–9,000**

▲ **A Vicenza-stone figure, Italian, 20th century**
This is an example of the modern taste for pretty carvings that are relatively affordable. **£1,500–2,500/ $2,250–3,750**

▲ **A Vicenza-stone figure of a girl holding a bird's nest, Italian, 20th century**
This kind of modern, and rather "cute", sculpture is popular today. **£1,500–2,500/ $2,250–3,750**

COMPOSITION STONE

Composition stone was invented by the Romans, but it was not until the 19th century that it was first used for garden ornament. It is moulded, and not carved, so many copies of the same figure can be produced quite cheaply. Once such a figure is established in a garden it is difficult to spot that it is not a carved-stone original. Pieces tend to be made with iron armatures – if these rust they will expand and can cause splits. Look for rust stains and cracks, which are sure signs that a piece needs attention.

▲ ▶ A pair of eagles, Austin & Seeley, 19th century
These are extremely well-modelled and are examples of a very traditional style of gatepier capital. They are imposing enough for a large house, but not so grand that they could not be used in a more modest setting.
£3,000–5,000/$4,500–7,500 (the pair)

▲ Figure of a shepherd boy, Austin & Seeley, mid-19th century
Austin & Seeley developed a unique mix for composition stone, with large pieces of stone aggregate visible. This is a typical Victorian interpretation of an earlier, less conveniently draped figure by Danish sculptor Thorwaldsen.
£5,000–8,000/$7,500–12,000

AUSTIN & SEELEY

Austin & Seeley were probably the earliest manufacturers of artificial stone, which they marketed as being of "light tint, which requires no painting or colouring, and will not sustain injury from the severest winter". Unlike the earlier Coade Stone Manufactory (*see* page 40), whose material was clay-based and fired in a kiln, Austin & Seeley's artificial stone was a cold-cast aggregate of large stone chips and mortar.

▶ **Figure of Eros,
Dutch, 20th century**
This winged figure,
symbolizing "Love", is very
familiar but surprisingly such
figures are not common,
which adds to their value.
£1,800–2,500/$2,700–3,750

◀ **A figure of a stork,
late 20th century**
This is a very popular subject
as a water bird is an obvious
ornament for a pond. The
stork figure shown here
should scare away herons
so that your fish are safe.
**£3,000–5,000/
$4,500–7,500**

▲ **A modern figure of a mother and child**
The mother has been romanticized by being
portrayed in Victorian dress, but this is not
an antique piece and probably dates to the
end of the 20th century. The subject matter
makes it popular and its small size (46cm/18in
tall) means that it can be included as part
of a scheme for a small garden.
£80–120/$120–180

TERRACOTTA & STONEWARE

The development of stoneware and terracotta so that they could be used for ornament made an enormous contribution to the existing market for statuary in the garden. When Eleanor Coade found a formula for fired clay that was resistant to frost it meant that very elaborate figures could be produced at relatively cheap prices (*see* box on page 40). Many of these classical figures are still in existence today and they retain the crispness that made them originally so popular.

◀ **A terracotta figure of Flora, Blashfield,** *c.*1850
This is a copy of the antique figure, Capitoline Flora – one of several such models produced by John Marriot Blashfield. It is made of a fired clay and is very durable. You will see that the forearms are missing; the original figure (carved in marble) held a posy of flowers in her left hand.
£3,000–5,000/$4,500–7,500

▲ **A rare terracotta model of a whippet, Blanchard,** *c.*1860
The base is stamped "Mark Terra Cotta M H Blanchard & Co, Blackfriars Road, London". Dogs are very popular as garden sculptures; there are many collectors of specific breeds, and whippets are particularly sought after.
£1,500–2,500/$2,250–3,750

BLANCHARD

Mark Blanchard served his apprenticeship with Coade and Sealy and then, in 1839, set up his own works in the Blackfriars Road, London, buying some of Coade's moulds. J.M. Blashfield, in his essay on terracotta, wrote that he was inspired by Blanchard's prize-winning work at the Great Exhibition of 1851. Although Blanchard later changed to a more fashionable, strongly coloured terracotta, some of his earlier pieces were indistinguishable from Coade's, apart from the maker's stamp.

Pieces displaying the Blashfield stamp command a premium in today's market.

▲ **A terracotta bacchante, Italian, late 20th century**
This is typical of imitation products of earlier pieces. Terracotta busts are not as sought after as those in other materials, such as marble, so are more affordable. **£250–350/$375–525**

◄ **A stoneware figure of a girl, late 19th/ early 20th century**
This decorative figure is typical of the sort of mass-produced stoneware appealing to those who have a taste for "pretty" ornament. It is not finely modelled, and does not bear close inspection, but it will do well tucked beside a flowering shrub or in a border, and is affordable. **£500–800/$750–1,200**

► **A pair of stoneware lions, *c.*1900**
This model is based on a design by Alfred Stevens (a 19th-century painter and decorative sculptor) and is widely copied. It can also be found in lead and composition stone. These lions were intended as gatepier finials, but could be used on a flight of steps or flanking a path. **£800–1,200/$1,200–1,800**

THE VALUE OF TERRACOTTA

Owing to the popularity of terracotta garden ornament in Europe and the USA throughout the 19th century, pieces can still be found for quite reasonable prices. There are notable 20th-century manufacturers who justifiably command high prices, and some who still produce pieces today. However, this abundance of antique terracotta means that little is being reproduced to such a high standard. Normally reproductions are in the cheaper composition stone, which should be easily identifiable when compared to the real thing.

BRONZE

Bronze has been used since Roman times and has always been popular. If it is kept outside it will attain a green/blue patina, and the longer the piece is exposed to the elements the deeper the patination. It is possible to have a statue coated so that the golden-brown colour of the bronze remains the same, but this is all a matter of taste as some people like patination while others prefer bronze in its original state. Cleaned, burnished bronze doesn't look natural in a garden and detracts from the value.

▲ A bronze figure of a faun holding an owl, after Clodion, *c.*1870
Claude Michel Clodion was a French sculptor active in the 18th century. This is a very appealing small sculpture – the base is also cast with owls, which perhaps refers to learning, as the young faun is just starting out on his quest for knowledge. The piece is only 30cm (12in) high, but is so well conceived that it makes a big impact.
£1,000–1,500/ $1,500–2,250

▼ A bronze figure of Mercury after the original by Giam Bologna, late 19th century
This model of the messenger to the gods is possibly the most popular garden sculpture and has been reproduced in practically any material you can think of, and in various sizes. This example is cast in bronze, and is 203cm (80in) in height, so it would fetch a high price at auction.
£6,000–10,000/$9,000–15,000

▲ A bronze figure of a heron, Donald Gilbert, 1937
This is a good example of animal sculpture of the period. Donald Gilbert was the son of Walter Gilbert, who started the Bromsgrove Guild of Applied Arts in 1898 (*see page 31*). This model was exhibited at the Royal Academy in 1938 as "1568 Heron-model for a bronze garden fountain".
£8,000–12,000/ $12,000–18,000

This detail shows the screwhead on the neck that joins the head to the body.

◄ Bronze crane, Japanese, late 19th century

At the turn of the 19th and 20th centuries there began a taste for Oriental gardens in England and this is an example of the kind of pieces that were made. There are modern reproductions being produced in Thailand and the Far East today; these have straight legs and the heads and necks are cast in one piece with the body. The original Japanese examples have separate heads that are screwed to the body at the base of the neck. **£2,000–3,000/$3,000–4,500**

▲ A pair of bronze temple dogs (shi-shi), Japanese, Meiji period (1868–1912)

It is quite rare to find these outside of Japan, although some pieces of this kind were transported to England by their owners, who had visited Japan. Originally set either side of a doorway to protect against evil spirits, these are just the kind of thing to give an Oriental feel to your garden.
£2,500–4,000/$3,750–6,000

SPOTTING A REAL BRONZE

Owing to the high prices they often achieve in today's market, bronzes are being reproduced both in solid metal and in resin, which has bronze powder mixed into it. As bronze was always a prestigious material the best craftsmen were employed in its manufacture, but resin copies can also be very good and hard to differentiate. A solid bronze piece should ring when tapped lightly with a hard object – resin will produce a dull sound. Real bronze is also heat resistant, whereas a resin piece will melt at a much lower temperature – a drastic test but definitive. A lot of bronzes are signed, so it is always worth checking for a signature.

LEAD & ZINC

In the 18th century lead statuary was usually painted in naturalistic colours so much of it would have been very garish to modern taste. Most existing lead statuary is 20th-century in date, and the modern taste is for the pieces to be left unpainted. Several foundries make reproductions of 18th-century originals, often to very high standards. Zinc, and the closely related alloy spelter, were most commonly used in the USA and Germany for garden ornament.

FAUNS & SATYRS

Most modern reproductions of Classical pieces are of goddesses, gods, and male and female figures, but there is a growing trend for something a little more sinister at the end of the garden. You can have a satyr (horned and with goat's legs) leering at you from behind a swathe of greenery, or why not have a faun (horned, with a small tail but with human feet), drunken and holding a wine skin?

▲ **Four lead figures depicting the Seasons, J.P. White, early 20th century**
Figures of the Seasons are very popular, and these are attractive examples. Lead is so heavy, and is such a soft material, that the weight of the heads tends to push them into the necks. Lead was a very popular material for garden statuary in the 18th century, but the Victorians preferred something more durable. However, the popularity of lead figures revived in the 20th century and various companies produced, and still do produce, a variety of garden statuary in lead.
£2,000–3,000/$3,000–4,500 (the set)

This is an example of what happens when the weight of the lead is supported on a slender column – in this case the neck.

▲ **Dancing Faun lead bust, 18th century**
This is attributed to John Cheere, who supplied a full-size lead copy for Castle Hill, Devon and a plaster model for Croome Court, Worcestershire in 1767.
£6,000–8,000/ $9,000–12,000

**▼ A pair of zinc-alloy deer,
American, late 19th century**

These have no manufacturer's stamp, but it is probable that they were produced by the Fiske Foundry. This type of naturalistic animal subject was popular in the USA, as it meant that owners could give the impression of having animals in their grounds without the attendant difficulties of dealing with livestock. The value is increased because they are American – you could get a similar European lead piece for a fraction of the cost.

£6,000–10,000/$9,000–15,000

**▲ A lead figure of a girl in 18th-century
dress, H. Crowther Ltd, 20th century**

This is a popular figure and is based on similar designs in lead created by John Cheere in the 18th century.

£1,000–1,500/$1,500–2,250

**▲ A lead figure of
Eros, 20th century**

There are many sculptures of the god of love but this is a particularly popular model.

£1,200–1,800/$1,800–2,700

**◄ A pair of lead figures
of reclining greyhounds,
late 20th century**

Dogs of any kind are popular ornaments and are often used on gatepiers flanking a gateway. Similar models in stoneware were produced by Blanchard (*see* page 84).

**£1,000–1,500/
$1,500–2,250**

CAST IRON

Most 19th-century cast-iron figures were produced in France. English foundries made figures as parts of fountains, or as pedestals, but a stand-alone figure is likely to have been produced in France. Of the French foundries, Val d'Osne and Barbezat were the most well-known. In 1858 Barbezat brought out a large catalogue showing designs for a huge range of cast-iron statuary, with a sizeable section devoted to anamalier subjects. Other countries produced cast-iron statuary, but none to such high standards.

◄ **Hippomene and Atalanta, J.J. Ducel Foundry, 19th century**
These are examples of the kinds of impressive piece produced by the Val d'Osne Foundry (which owned Ducel) in France. Atalanta was an athletic huntress who challenged any potential suitor to a race, the penalty for the loser being death. She was unbeaten until Hippomene challenged her; this pair of figures shows their race. He dropped three golden apples given to him by Venus; Atalanta could not resist picking them up, and lost the race as a result. **£10,000–15,000/$15,000–22,500**

▶ **A reclining hound, French, late 19th century**
The model is supposed to be of a hound, but someone with an inventive turn of mind has used a pot of paint to turn it into a dalmatian. This treatment has not enhanced the value, and if you wanted to sell such an item you should first remove the modern finish.
£2,500–4,000/$3,750–6,000

▶ **A cast-iron figure of the young Bacchus, entitled "Buveur", after Hippolyte Moreau, French, late 19th century**

Hippolyte Moreau was a prolific 19th-century French sculptor. Bacchus is a popular subject for garden sculpture; the model here is life-size and would make a good central point in a garden. This particular figure is painted black, but cast iron is often painted white to resemble marble.

£4,000–6,000/$6,000–9,000

▲ **A cast-iron jockey tethering post, American, late 19th century**

This figure is stamped "McKittrick Foundry Co., Union Beach, N.J.". American pieces are much sought after as the market for garden statuary in the USA is still an expanding one and American items are preferred. These jockey tethering posts were often painted with the racing colours of the owners.

£1,000–1,500/ $1,500–2,250

The vertical casting line on the lion's stomach.

◀ **One of a pair of cast-iron figures of lions, American, late 19th/early 20th century**

These lions have been cast in two halves. They were probably used as gatepiers or seen on a parapet, where the casting line would not have been so visible.

£3,000–5,000/ $4,500–7,500 (the pair)

CLASSICAL FIGURES

If you are wishing to research the figure in your garden, you can refer here to a selection of the most commonly copied models that you will normally encounter. The originals range in date from Roman Imperial times through the Renaissance to the 18th century. As you will see, the uniting theme is that they are all based on Classical ideals. As a result they have enjoyed enduring popularity – so much so that the majority of them are still being reproduced today.

Apollo Belvedere

Arrotino

Cupid and Psyche

Dancing Faun with cymbals

Dancing Faun

Diana la Chasseresse

Diana de Gabies

Discobolus

Farnese Flora

Farnese Hercules

Mercury after Giam Bologna

Seated Mercury

The Dying Gladiator

Pair of reclining lions in the style of Canova

Minerva Giustiniani

Narcissus

Silenus and the Infant Bacchus

The Spinaro

Callipygian Venus

Venus after Canova

Capitoline Venus

Crouching Venus

Venus de Milo

Venus de Medici

Winged Victory of Samothrace

Warwick Vase

ARCHITECTURAL ORNAMENT

There is a wealth of architectural salvage on the market that can be used as decoration in a garden. When old buildings are demolished many of the ornamental features come onto the market and it is fun to scout around some of the architectural salvage yards looking for a special piece. Most affordable pieces will date to the 19th or early 20th century. The taste for "modern" housing in the 1960s meant that a great many Victorian and Edwardian houses were either demolished or remodelled, which resulted in an abundance of ornament ending up in salvage yards. At the present time the recycling of earlier architectural ornament has not travelled to the USA, but its popularity will probably spread there in the coming years. However, staddle stones are one exception – once largely unknown in the USA, they have now been searched out and incorporated into American garden design, usually to edge a pathway or surround a lawn.

It is easy to accommodate these pieces in your garden – you just need a bit of lateral thinking: for example, what was once a carved stone doorway could easily be placed on the ground and used as a pool surround, with a wall as the backing; a gargoyle head can be used as a wall fountain; elaborate ceiling roses can be painted and used as roundels to decorate a plain wall; and a flight of steps could be recycled as a base for a water cascade. When you look around a garden centre and see what is being charged for a piece of rock the size of your fist, you will realize that items from salvage yards are relatively cheap and worth investigating.

Some people like to use old agricultural machinery as ornaments – the carved stone troughs once used for farm animals to drink from are now sought after as garden features. The popularity of barn conversions has meant that these rustic troughs have increased in value recently: an old stone drinking trough, 190cm (75in) in length, can fetch as much as £1,200 ($1,800) at auction today, whereas it would have made only £250 ($375) ten years ago.

MARBLE

Marble is an expensive material and was therefore used in moderation as architectural decoration. It is possible to find troughs of marble, but on the whole marble architectural fittings will have come from a church or chapel. However, for this very reason, the quality of carving to be found in marble fittings is likely to be much finer than carving done in stone, and fragments from ecclesiastical buildings are not expensive. So, if you have the imagination to reuse existing carvings, you could save a lot of money.

▲ A large, white-marble mortar, probably 18th century
Originally mortars were intended for use in the making of medicines and ointments – the tapered shape makes them ideal for the crushing of solids into powder. They were also used in kitchens for the preparation of sauces and to crush herbs. These days a mortar makes an ideal plant holder, or filled with water can be used as a bird bath – the side lugs make suitable platforms for the thirsty birds.
£600–1,000/$900–1,500

▲ A grey-marble cistern, French, 18th century
Once used to collect rainwater, modern buyers would probably convert this for use as either a fountain or a planter. It would look great raised up onto a pedestal.
£1,000–1,500/$1,500–2,250

This veining is typical of French grey marble.

◄ A pair of carved Istrian-stone wall troughs, late 19th century
Istrian stone is a kind of hard granite, almost marble, which comes from Italy. These rustic-looking wall troughs would be a good addition to a patio, or even against the wall of a small garden.
£1,000–1,500/$1,500–2,250

STONE

In recent years the inclusion of a variety of pieces of architectural ornament in garden design has become fashionable again. Owing to the housing boom in the 1960s, many Victorian and Edwardian houses were either demolished or remodelled and their architectural features removed. These found their way to architectural salvage yards. Natural stone is one of the most suitable materials for use in the garden, as stone ornament can take on new life in a garden setting.

▲ A set of four Portland-stone staddle stones
These stones have tapering square stems, which are more popular than cylindrical ones. They are also nicely weathered and have a sprinkling of lichen, which adds to their value.
£600–1,000/$900–1,500 (the set)

▲ A pair of unusually large Cotswold-stone staddle stones
The generous size and weathering, complete with mossy tops, of these stones means they would fetch a high price at auction.
£1,000–1,500/$1,500–2,250

▲ Two pairs of staddle stones
The first pair are particularly tall and could be used at an entrance or a gateway. Although all four staddle stones have the popular square stem, they are a little too clean to make a high price. **Tall pair: £400–600/$600–900 Smaller pair: £300–400/$450–600**

STADDLE STONES

Staddle stones are very popular today as garden decoration. Their original use was to support wooden barns above the ground so that rats could not get at the grain inside. Most of the examples on the market today are from the 19th century, but it is difficult to date them precisely as staddle stones have been made in the same way since the 16th century. Their value has increased greatly recently – the most sought after being large and well-weathered. Square-stemmed ones are more popular than cylindrical ones. The most desirable stone is Cotswold because, like other similar limestones, it weathers with a rich variety of lichens and mosses.

TRANSPORTING STONE ITEMS

One thing to remember if you are thinking of buying large stone items is their enormous weight. It is no use going to collect six staddle stones in an ordinary car, as stone weighs approximately 160lb (72.5kg) per cubic foot. You would need to use a van, and should also make sure that you have help to load and unload the items from the vehicle.

▼ **Two sandstone troughs, early 20th century**
The value of these oval troughs depends upon condition. A particularly fine example, such as the one on the right, could make up to £4,000 ($6,000) at auction. If you want your trough to grow mosses and lichens like this, then keep it in a damp corner of the garden away from full sunlight.
Left: £1,000–1,500/$1,500–2,250
Right: £3,000–4,000/$4,500–6,000

◄ **One of a pair of stone capitals, middle-European, 18th century**
Some salvage yards specialize in garden and architectural ornament and have a great variety of pieces available. These carved decorations, once set upon pillars, have retained the crispness of the carving, probably because they were protected by a porch or portico. Pieces of this kind are still cheap to buy. They can be used as ornaments on their own or as supports, perhaps for a bench or to hold a trough.
£600–1,000/$900–1,500 (the pair)

▲ A rustic stone trough, French, late 18th/early 19th century

This is a very rustic example, and is probably just a carved-out lump of rock, but it looks very effective planted out with flowers. **£200–300/$300–450**

▼ A large red sandstone trough, late 19th century

This started life as a feed trough for animals but could be planted out along the side of a driveway. **£1,000–1,500/$1,500–2,250**

▲ Stone trough, French, probably 18th century

This was once a wellhead, as can be seen from the remains of the rusty pump that is still fitted to the end of the trough. It was probably used for watering animals. These troughs used to be seen in every French village, but because they now have a commercial value they are often replaced by composition stone planters. The original troughs are either moved to more secure environments or sold to salvage yards. **£2,000–3,000/$3,000–4,500**

The holes in the top of this wellhead show that the cast-iron pump is a replacement, probably 19th century.

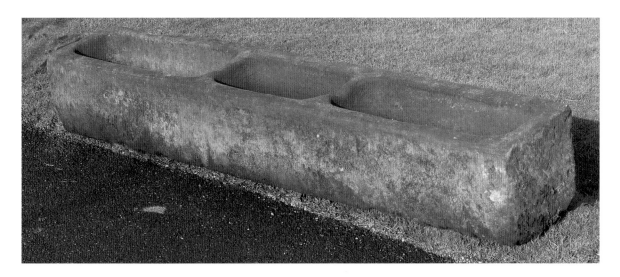

LEAD

Until the mid-20th century the majority of domestic plumbing, including gutters, downpipes, and flashings, was all made of lead. This began to be replaced by cast iron once it was readily available as it was cheaper and could be cast with more intricate patterns. In the latter part of the 20th century it became known that using lead as a receptacle for drinking water was a health hazard, so most lead pipes were replaced. Today these attractive features can be picked up quite cheaply.

▲ **Set of five lead rainwater hoppers and pipe heads**
These were once completely utilitarian, but nowadays people plant them with trailing plants and fix them to their walls. They can also be adapted for use as wall fountains. Do not be put off by splits, or the fact that a hopper is misshapen, because the restoration of lead is relatively cheap as it is such a soft material. **£50–150/$75–225 (each)**

▲ A working lead pump
This is typical, in both construction and design, of pumps produced from the 18th century right up until the 20th century. Pumps like this were common in villages and on farms. **£60–100/$90–150**

▲ Selection of hoppers, late 19th century
The very decorative hopper (bottom left) is in fact made of cast iron; most hoppers are lead, but some were made of iron.
£50–120/$75–180 each
(£100/$150 for the cast-iron hopper)

◄ A rare parish boundary plaque, early 19th century
This sort of plaque is believed to have been used to mark out parish boundaries.
£100–150/$150–225

◄ Two washing coppers, early 20th century
These coppers, originally used in kitchens for boiling clothes, are now popular as garden planters. Some of the larger ones are big enough to be used as pots to hold small trees.
Small copper:
£300–500/$450–750
Large copper:
£500–800/$750–1,200

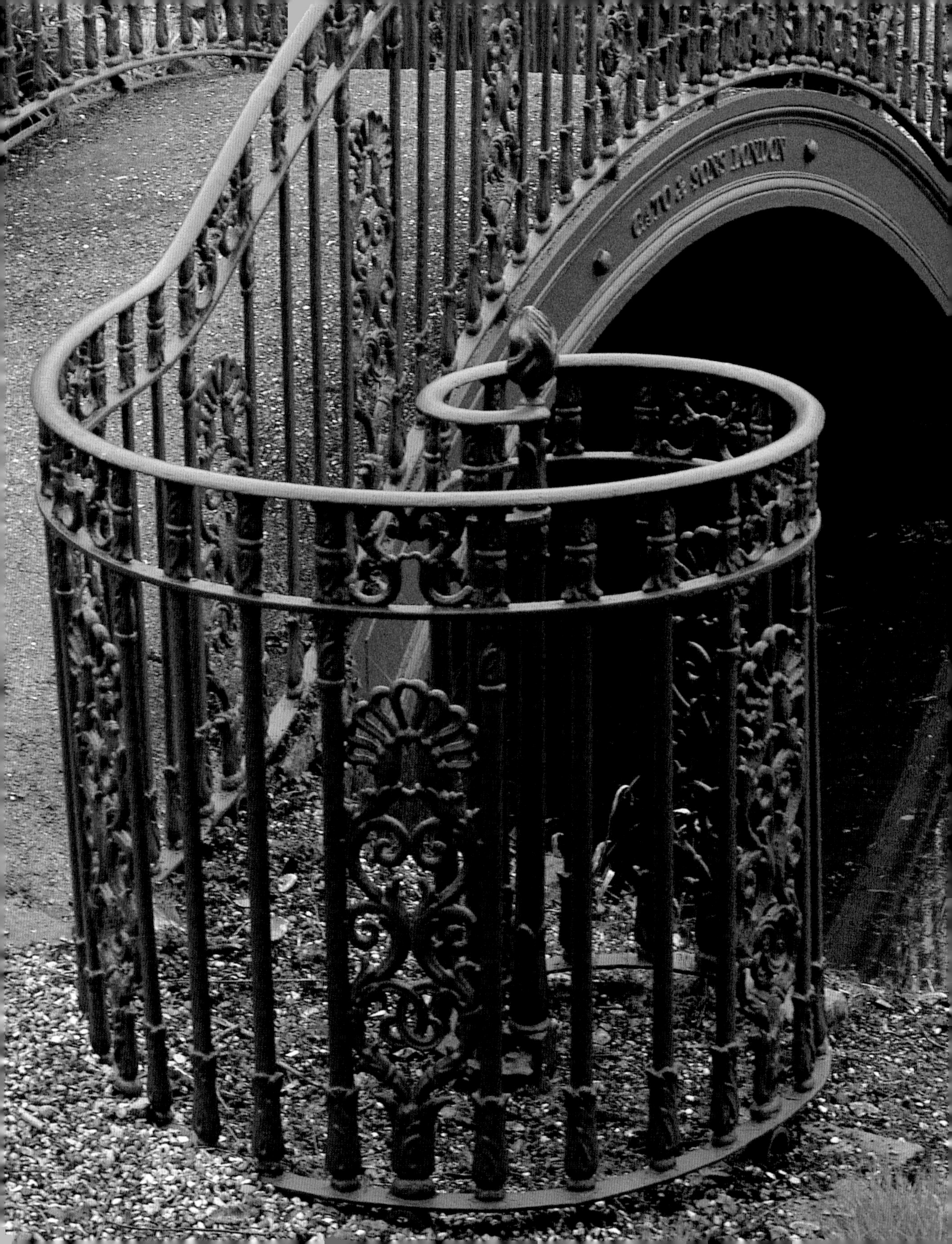

STRUCTURES

The single thing that will make the most impact in a garden design is some kind of garden structure. This sounds expensive, but with a little imagination it is possible to construct a temple or a gazebo for a modest outlay. Such a structure is, after all, just a few columns with a roof of some sort; unless you want it in carved stone or marble the cost will be mainly in the labour. If you can do it yourself then you could make something very impressive without breaking the bank.

Maybe a temple would look out of place in a small garden, but summer houses are making a comeback. Designed originally for use in sanatoriums, the revolving summer house was very popular in England in the early part of the 20th century. The wooden structure sat on a circle of grooved metal and could be pushed round 360 degrees so that it always faced the sun. Boulton & Paul, based in Norwich, England, made a selection of these revolving summer houses and called them "Sunshine Rooms"; many are still in use today.

A structure need not be a building at all, as there are other ways of making a statement with one object. You could consider an obelisk, which would draw the eye upwards, or install a row of chimney pots. A very large number of terracotta chimney pots are available on the market today and they come in all shapes and sizes. The plain ones can be purchased for under £100 ($150) whereas the very decorative "crown" pots, some dating back to the 17th century, are considerably more expensive. This is because they are quite rare due to the fact that buildings of that age are listed, and therefore protected.

If you have an existing building in your garden, the garage or a shed for example, you could enhance it by the addition of a weather vane. These are very attractive, can tell you the direction of the wind so that you know who is going to get the smoke when you light your bonfire, and are readily available. Victorian weather vanes are not expensive, and can make a big statement. When using structures in the garden you should not be fainthearted – less is not always more and, in some cases, size really does matter.

ORIENTAL STRUCTURES

In the 1870s a fashion for Oriental gardens began in Europe, which reached its height in the 1930s. A quantity of carved granite lanterns, wooden bridges, and other Oriental ornaments found its way to England and, to a lesser extent, to the Continent. These structures are still quite popular today – the large stone lanterns, called "kasuge" lanterns, make an exotic change from European ornaments, and the classic Chinese bridge can be a very attractive point of interest in any garden.

◄ **Oriental-style lantern, English, early 20th century**
This fantastic concoction is an exuberant manifestation of the popularity of the Japanese garden in England at the time. The piece is sectional, so it can be built up in the same way as a tower of bricks, but it is not very stable. Original Japanese lanterns were never of this size: this is most definitely a European interpretation of Oriental taste.
£1,000–1,500/$1,500–2,250

► **Carved granite lantern, Oriental, probably 19th century**
Because granite is so hard it does not weather in the same way as sandstone or limestone, and so it is difficult to tell exactly how old such pieces are. £3,000–5,000/$4,500–7,500

This clean granite shows a lack of weathering.

▲ Lanterns, English, 1930s
Original Japanese lanterns are much more valuable than these English copies, which make the mistake of having no "cage" at the centre so they cannot be used as lanterns at all. The values given for these pieces reflect this fault.
£1,000–1,500/$1,500–2,250 (each)

▲ A bronze lantern, Japanese, Meiji period
This lantern is set with bells that sound when the wind blows. It is designed to light a person's way and to ward off evil spirits.
£2,000–3,000/$3,000–4,500

▲ A granite kasuge lantern, Japanese, Meiji period (1868–1912)
This lantern originally was made for a Japanese market. However, the popularity of Oriental design meant that lanterns of a very similar kind began to be imported into England. **£2,500–3,000/$3,750–4,500**

▲ Modern bridge based on a traditional Chinese design, English, 20th century
The European interest in Oriental gardens has not waned, and this bridge would make an important contribution to an Oriental theme. Chinese bridges of this kind were always painted red, so you would not get the same effect if you were to paint it any other colour.
£2,000–3,000/$3,000–4,500

ROTUNDAS & GAZEBOS

Ever since gardens were first established people have set up various structures within them – some for shelter and others for pure decoration. The designs of these creations were often based on the whim of the owner, and made to order by local craftsmen. Today modern structures can be bought direct from the manufacturer, but of course these do look brand new. Most buyers still want a structure to look as if it has been in their garden for years, so a premium is paid for antique examples.

▲ **A stone pergola, Italian, 20th century**
This is made up of stone columns with a modern wooden top. Stone columns can be purchased from architectural yards at a fraction of the cost of newly carved columns. Alternatively, you could get a very similar look by buying composition-stone columns and having your local carpenter make the woodwork at the top. Once you have planted such a structure with climbing roses or honeysuckle it will look fabulous.
Stone: £6,000–10,000/$9,000–15,000
Composition stone: £3,000–5,000/$4,500–7,500

◄ **A carved Vicenza-stone rotunda, Italian, 20th century**
This piece was made in Vicenza and then imported to the UK. As it is such a heavy piece the shipping would have been very expensive, which affects the overall price.
£8,000–12,000/
$12,000–18,000

▲ **A wirework gazebo, early 20th century**
Wirework was very popular in Victorian times. However, its popularity has begun to wane so gazebos of this kind are relatively affordable today. **£800–1,200/$1,200–1,800**

GAZEBOS, TEMPLES, & ROTUNDAS

If you have set your heart on a temple, gazebo, or rotunda, and do not have the necessary funds to buy one "off the shelf" from a modern retailer, it is worth considering that they are only a collection of columns with some kind of roof or latticed woodwork. You can get the same effect by purchasing old columns from an architectural salvage yard and having them erected in your garden beneath a suitable top. Large architectural pieces like columns are not easy to sell, so you may well discover a bargain. Such an approach also has the advantage of being flexible, as you can create your own design or change it to fit what is available. For instance, if you find five columns you can make a five-sided gazebo.

When setting up your structure you obviously do not want it to fall down again in the first thunderstorm so the columns should be properly set into the ground and the joints mortared together.

It is difficult to find original 19th-century gazebos and temples because they are usually kept *in situ*, but if you are lucky enough to find one you will have to pay a premium for its established "weathered" look.

▲ **A wrought-iron gazebo, by Cotswold Decorative Ironwork, 20th century**
This gazebo is made of panels, some incorporating earlier wrought iron. The piece is modular, making it easy to erect. A gazebo is a popular garden feature, and the price quoted reflects this fact.
£1,500–2,000/ $2,250–3,000

OBELISKS & CHIMNEY POTS

The use of obelisks as garden ornaments can be traced back to antiquity, and expeditions to Egypt in the 18th and early 19th centuries popularized them as decorative features. Their attraction lies in the fact that they work well as vista pieces, or at the junction of views. They can be found in all sizes, from small gatepiers to those that are 3–4m (10–13ft) tall. Chimney pots were available from Elizabethan times but probably were not used as garden ornaments until the Victorian era. They can be used for forcing vegetables or holding plants, and are popular in the USA as well as in Europe.

◀ **A pair of small Vicenza obelisks, Italian, late 20th century**
These obelisks are each set on four balls and a square pedestal. They would be perfect for flanking a gateway into an Italian-style garden, or to give some height to a border.
£2,500–4,000/ $3,750–6,000 (the pair)

▲ **A granite obelisk, 20th century**
This Egyptian-style obelisk would look good situated in the middle of a rose garden as it is 312cm (123in) in height.
£3,000–5,000/$4,500–7,500

HISTORY OF OBELISKS

An obelisk is a tapering pillar of stone, originally erected by the Egyptians who placed them in pairs before the portals of temples. The base was traditionally one tenth of the height, and the obelisks were carved with hieroglyphics. The best-known one in Britain is Cleopatra's Needle, which stands on the Embankment in London. The pleasing dimensions of obelisks means that they are popular features today and therefore attract high prices. The basic shape has also been adapted into many different designs. Often the stone obelisk sits on four spheres on a square base but the obelisk shape can also be found in trellised plant supports, or echoed in topiary.

◀ **A collection of terracotta chimney pots, 1880–1900**
These can be used in a variety of ways in the garden. You can plant them out, use them as forcing pots for rhubarb, or as pedestals for sculptures. There are a lot of them on the market so they are quite affordable.
£80–120/$120–180 (each)

◀ **A terracotta chimney pot, late 19th century**
The more attractive a chimney pot is the more money it fetches, and this is a good example of a pleasing design.
£120–150/$180–225

CHIMNEY POTS

Many of the 19th-century stoneware chimney pots were decorated in tremendous detail, especially considering they were designed to be on rooftops. The enormous number of pots that were made means that today they are not expensive – good-quality examples can be found easily for under £150 ($225). This makes them a very attractive prospect, especially when you compare that price with the cost of the best stoneware urns.

SUMMER HOUSES

The summer house is a particularly English phenomenon. Other countries have chalets or hunting lodges, but the English love their summer houses. Most of these date to the beginning of the 20th century and, as they were made of wood, many of them have deteriorated. An original early 20th-century summer house can set you back a few thousand pounds/dollars, but they are still being manufactured today so it is possible to obtain a modern one at far less cost.

▲ **An Edwardian rustic summer house, early 20th century**
There is no maker's name on this summer house, but it is similar to the example on the left and so is likely to have been made by Barnard, Bishop and Barnard.
£3,000–5,000/$4,500–7,500

▲ **A rustic summer house, Barnard, Bishop and Barnard, early 20th century**
This company produced a huge range of garden furniture and ornaments. The rustic exterior and lancet-shaped windows are examples of a design that was popular in the 1920s and '30s.
£4,000–6,000/$6,000–9,000

▶ **A revolving summer house, probably by Boulton & Paul, early 20th century**
This summer house can be moved 360 degrees so that it always faces the direction of the sun.
£1,500–2,500/ $2,250–3,750

The value of this summer house is increased by the painting and furnishing of the interior.

▲ **A Boulton & Paul summer house, early 20th century**
This summer house bears the maker's plaque above the door, and has been lovingly restored. The interior has been fitted out with furniture and paintings and it is tempting to imagine whiling away a summer's afternoon lazing in one of the chairs, with the veranda always facing the sun. The mechanism of these summer houses is very simple but effective: even a child could push the building round in a full circle.
£2,000–3,000/$3,000–4,500

BOULTON & PAUL

Boulton & Paul were based in Norfolk. They were originally involved in aircraft manufacture, but began to make a wide range of garden furniture and summer houses after World War I, up until the late 20th century. The summer house shown on this page is one of a type known as "Sunshine Rooms" – so-called because they were used in sanatoriums for tuberculosis patients. It was understood that sunshine was part of the cure, and because the summer house revolved it meant the patient could always be in sunshine. Such rooms were built to the highest quality.

WEATHER VANES

It is not known when weather vanes first became decorative, rather than purely functional, objects. The Tudors had intricately worked vanes, but the tradition may stretch back a lot further than the 16th century. The most valuable examples are American vanes – although they are identical to European ones in construction and often motifs, an American vane backed up by provenance is worth many times its European counterpart in the USA today, as the market there is so strong.

◄ **A typical wrought- and cast-iron weather vane, 1880**
This is a good example of the basic design with the direction points, N,S,E, and W, below an arrow pointer. The heavy construction has assured this vane's survival to the present day.
£600–1,000/$900–1,500

► **A wrought-iron weather vane, late 19th century**
This has been adapted by the recent addition of a cut-out butterfly. It is an example of how a plain weather vane can be transformed into a highly desirable object just by the use of a little imagination.
£1,000–1,500/$1,500–2,250

► **A sheet-copper weather vane, c.1905**
The wrought-iron support is here surmounted by a sheet-copper galleon. This is a "one-off" weather vane, probably made to order, and is an example of the high quality that is available. Vanes can be found with a variety of cut-out terminals – a ship is a popular choice.
£2,000–3,000/ $3,000–4,500

AMERICAN WEATHER VANES

The reason for the great disparity in value between European and American vanes lies purely in market forces. American buyers, looking for something with a good provenance dating back a century or so, will pay almost anything for this tangible proof of American history. For example, in July 2002 a late 19th-century American weather vane in the form of a steam locomotive sold for more than $240,000 (£160,000) at auction. However, to obtain such huge prices it is vital to have proof of provenance and some history of the piece.

BRIDGES

Until the 20th century private bridges would only have been found in estates or parks. Before the Industrial Revolution people who needed bridges had them made by the estate blacksmiths or stonemasons, but once it was possible to have them made in cast iron they could be designed around existing railings, and were more easily obtained. Such structures are not cheap to buy today but, if you are lucky enough to have a stream or a lake, one could make a pleasing addition to your garden.

◄ **A cast-iron bridge, Val d'Osne Foundry, French, late 19th century**
Bridges of this kind are not often available for sale, as they mostly remain *in situ*. They therefore command high prices. **£8,000–12,000/ $12,000–18,000**

Val d'Osne Foundry mark

► **A smaller, rustic, composition-stone bridge, French, mid-20th century**
This is only 104cm (41in) in length and so could be used in a small garden. The naturalistic design makes it compatible with modern landscaping.
£800–1,200/$1,200–1,800

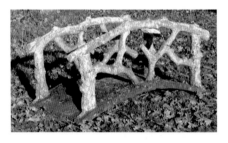

◄ **A modern wrought- and cast-iron bridge, by Cotswold Decorative Ironwork, late 20th century**
This is based on a 19th-century design and it even incorporates late 19th-century railings to good effect too.
£3,000–5,000/ $4,500–7,500

IMPLEMENTS
& ACCESSORIES

The earliest garden implements were robustly made, and evolved from agricultural tools whose origins are lost in pre-history. These tools were developed from the simplest forked stick or animal bone, and some were likely to have been used as much for hunting or fighting as for cultivation. From the Middle Ages there exist visual records of a familiar but limited range of tools for the gardener, such as a spade, mattock, hoe, and knife.

As the popularity of gardening accelerated in the 16th and 17th centuries, property owners began to appreciate the need for more specialized implements to achieve their required results. There were no commercial manufacturers from whom these items might be ordered, so village blacksmiths or skilled estate workers made them up by following drawings from the latest gardening books, while armourers probably made the more sophisticated implements. Consequently, by the mid-17th century the basic range of tools had been extended to include the fork, shears, pruning saw, rake, loppers, and a form of garden trowel. In America, the 17th-century tools that had travelled over with colonists began to be adapted and altered.

Certain tools and accessory items developed throughout the 18th century, but the greatest change occurred in the 19th century as a result of an emerging middle class with wealth and aspirations, and the competition offered through the advances of the Industrial Revolution. In the space of a few years the blacksmith's role became one of repairer only.

All this meant that basic tools were relatively cheap, although the purchase of certain implements, such as brass syringes, probably represented a more serious investment. Indeed, for the gentleman or lady gardener some particularly fine, small implements were available from high-class retailers, and these are particularly sought after by collectors today.

The demand for gardening tools increased in line with the growing love of gardening, and, although interrupted by World War I, production of this amazing variety of items lasted until the middle of the 20th century.

TOOLS

Anyone interested in collecting gardening tools can do so with a minimum of outlay. There are still large numbers of small hand tools – trowels, hand forks, and secateurs – that can be picked up very cheaply. Many of these will date from the early to mid-20th century, when a great variety of styles and sizes of tool was still being produced. Although some examples will be stamped with the name of the manufacturer, many are not, or the name has worn away over time. The collector may have to research old catalogues to identify the source – these catalogues are in themselves collectable, and are becoming scarce. They are invaluable for the serious collector, so it is worth looking out for them.

▲ **A bulb planter,** *c.*1920
This tool was specially designed for planting daffodil and other bulbs into grass. The manufacturers advertised it by saying "it cuts and lifts cleanly a piece of turf which can easily be replaced".
£40–60/$60–90

▲ **Spade,** *c.*1910
The larger hand tools, including spades, forks, and hoes, come in a fascinating range of shapes, each derived from a region or a specialist need that may have developed over hundreds of years. To call a spade just a "spade" would be too simplistic – this was a ground-breaking spade.
£50–80/$75–120

▲ **"Eezidigga"** *c.*1910
This is a form of "mule" spade that, according to the advertising of the time, "transforms labour into a pleasant exercise".
£60–100/$90–150

◄ Range of hoes, late 19th century to 1940
Hoes come in a wide variety of shapes, reflecting the preference for either thrusting or drawing movements during weeding. Popular styles are the "Dutch", "swan-neck", and "Canterbury", and other types include the "Spanish", "Plantation", and "Triangular".
£10–30/$15–45 (each)

▼ Shears, English and French, centre and left: 19th century; right: early 20th century
Shears for clipping hedges also came in an interesting variety of styles. In common use from the 17th century the basic product is fully recognizable today, although it has become much lighter. **£10–40/$15–60 (each)**

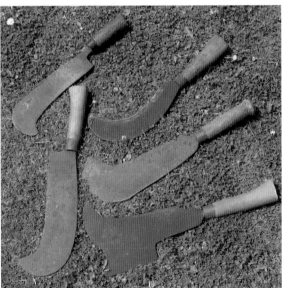

▲ Bill hooks
These instruments have been used for centuries for heavy pruning, hedging, and coppicing. There is a wide variety of regional shapes, as you can see from this selection. A number of early (18th/19th-century) types may be found with makers' stamps or marks. **£5–25/$8–38 (each)**

▲ Various pruning knives, small ones are English, larger French, late 19th/early 20th century
One of the gardener's most necessary implements, the folding knife came into favour in the early 19th century. Good-quality blades are often by Sheffield makers. **£10–30/$15–45 (each)**

▼ Hedge clipper, Ridgeways, *c.*1890–1920
The Victorians, in their wish to make everything easier, devised the Ridgeways "multi-clipper", which continued being produced well into the early 20th century.
£40–60/$60–90

▲ The "Myticuttah", an unusual pruning implement, 1930
Known as the "Myticuttah", this powerful pruner was used for grooming trees and shrubs.
£20–40/$30–60

CARE OF TOOLS

Many antique garden tools can still be used today. Larger tools such as spades and forks may still give excellent service, though they can be heavier to use than modern examples and require a little looking after. Advice from early 20th-century writers recommends that after use most metal tools should be scraped clean and wiped with a wet rag, followed by an oily rag. One writer stated: "Each (tool) should have its allotted space in the tool shed and invariably be put back after use." Many old tools will not have received such respect, but will still look better after a gentle rub with an emery cloth and a good wax polish.

▲ Range of forks and trowels, late 19th/early 20th century
Perhaps the most popular area of interest for collectors is smaller hand tools, of which there is a huge variety available to choose from. Many of these can still be used or attractively displayed. These hand forks and trowels were made for both general and specialist use.
£3–15/$5–23 (each)

▲ Hedge clipper, 1920s
In the late 1920s the amazing "Little Wonder" one- or two-man hedge clipper was making a rather brief appearance. It is rare to find an example in its original wooden storage box and this increases its value considerably.
£250–350/$375–525

◄ A selection of daisy grubbers, late 19th/ early 20th century
Operating on a fulcrum these implements were designed for lifting weeds, particularly daisies. The selection here covers slightly differing forms but they are all based on the same design. The largest example was designed for digging up dockleaves.
£5–35/$8–55 (each)

▶ **A collection of small hand tools, 19th/20th century**

These are all for raking and cultivating, and the range includes an unusual claw-shaped tool, c.1925, and a dual-purpose implement for digging and raking. The tool on the left of the picture is a "spud" – one of the earliest types of weeding implement. It is mentioned in Samuel Pepys' diaries of the 1660s, but this example dates to the late 19th century. The origin of the name "spud", now associated with potatoes, is not known but was used to refer to broad-bladed digging implements. Note the implement made with bent nails, which dates to the 1940s – this is an example of a tool that looks almost hand-made but was in fact manufactured inexpensively.
£5–25/$8–38 (each)

◀ **Range of secateurs, French and English, 1870–1930**

For pruning the French have provided the secateur – an indispensable implement that supplanted British pruning shears in the late 19th century. This tool again offers a wonderful array of shapes and sizes to the collector.
£5–25/$8–38 (each)

These shears were made in Sheffield, and have handles stamped with "FOR DADDY'S HELPER".

▲ **Range of children's tools, 20th century**
To introduce children to gardening, tools were made for them from the earliest years of the 20th century. These included watering cans and wheelbarrows, as well as spades, rakes, trowels, forks, and shears.
£5–15/$8–25 (each)

▲ **Toy lawn mower, Dinky Toys, c.1950**
This toy lawn mower has a rotating cutter and detachable grass box. It was totally out of scale compared with other models in the Dinky Toys range.
£25–35/$38–53

◀ **Child's mower, Webb, c.1955**
If you like the idea of collecting gardening-related pieces but have practically no space, you could consider a few children's tools. The Webb child's mower is simply a scaled-down working replica of one of the most popular adult models by Webb from the same era.
£80–140/$120–210

▶ **Garden lines**

Garden lines (or reels) are used for setting
out a garden, or merely a row of vegetables.
The frames can be found in metal or wood;
attractive wrought-iron examples date back
to the 18th century, and mass-produced ones
from the second part of the 19th century.
The frame is normally the most attractive
part, and the cord may be a replacement,
but it is better if the pin appears to be
original. Many pins have become separated
over the years and so lines are often found
with replacements.
£15–30/$25–45 (each)

◀ **Metal labels, early 20th century**

Plant labels, or tallies, would have originated
from wooden pegs carved with numbers
rather than plant names. The wider choice
of plants (many being introduced by plant
hunters in the 19th century), and the need
to identify plants and species, was behind
the introduction of such accessories. Initially
attractive ceramic examples were available,
but they later also appeared in stamped
metal. The examples shown here are made
of white metal and zinc and were available
with stems or pierced for suspension, as shown.
£5–10/$8–15 (each)

► **Syringes, 20th century**

The syringe was a 19th-century idea for spraying water and insecticides. The fact that the items were usually brass, and often well engineered, meant that they were originally relatively expensive. Popular British makers such as Abol and Four Oaks retailed at the higher end of the market. Shown right are a Four Oaks No. 1 51cm (20in) "Undentable" c.1920, a scarce Abol Junior of similar date, and a Dronwall from the mid-20th century. Pre-1900 examples are now difficult to find.

£10–30/$15–45 (each)

Abol Junior stamp

The Wikeham stamp

▲ **A "weed eradicator", Wikeham, 1915**

This rather ruthless-looking "Weed Eradicator" is a brass-bodied tool that is capable of delivering poison to a weed by means of its "needle". Implements like this that perform a specific purpose are becoming increasingly popular with collectors.

£80–120/$120–180

▲ **Flower and fruit gatherer, Dubois, 1910**

There are some items that do not fit easily into the category of tools, such as this flower and fruit gatherer – a trigger-operated implement for cutting and retrieving "out of reach" produce.

£100–150/$150–225

WATERING CANS & WATERING EQUIPMENT

One of the necessities when maintaining a garden is a good source of water. Watering cans made of metal were introduced around the end of the 17th century; prior to this, pottery was the favoured material. Notable centres of production for copper and brass cans were France and Holland. In the 19th century improved manufacturing techniques saw the introduction of tinplate and steel cans. From the 1930s–50s, when the production of the "perfect" lawn was almost an obsession, the use of sprinklers became popular. Simple forms of these early sprinklers are available today at reasonable prices.

WATERING CANS

The idea of painting a watering can may be fun, but this can spoil the item and vastly reduce its value. Most collectors wouldn't mind seeing old paint decoration on a can, but a recent repainting job would spoil the antique look.

Watering cans should not be confused with hot-water cans, which appear in copper and brass, and steel, and which have hinged lids. They were never intended to be used for gardening and were not produced with a rose spout.

From a collector's perspective, the variety of cans appearing on today's market from the Continent (notably France, Germany, Hungary, and Spain) is making this field a diverse and fascinating one.

▲ **Copper watering can, French, late 18th/early 19th century**
The French may be credited with producing the greatest variety of watering cans. In the 18th and early 19th centuries copper was the popular metal for this "classic" style of French can, which incorporated the "rose" within the spout. Although the example shown is well used (and repaired), it is still an attractive piece for a collector.
£400–600/$600–900

▼ Three early 20th-century cans
The two cans on the right are certainly French, but the more unusual one on the left is of much heavier gauge metal and is possibly Continental too. In line with many other "decorative" items, large numbers of French watering cans have been taken over to the UK by collectors in recent years. **£25–45/$38–68 (each)**

▲ Three tinplate and steel cans, French, late 19th century
After copper and brass came tinplate and steel cans. These three examples show the differing regional styles of French can. Note the can on the lower right of the photograph – an early example of a style still popular today. **£30–60/$45–90 (each)**

► A selection of watering cans, Haws, 20th century
Note the larger can with "japanned" finish, which is from the early to mid-20th century and is worth more because of this finish. A Haws product is more easily identified by the company trademark, which has their name and the current address and is found on the shoulder of the can.
£15–50/$23–75 (each)

▲ Pluviette sprinkler, French, early 20th century
The Victorians had garden hoses and all kinds of attachments
for directing water, and some attractive hose reels can
also be found. Lawns were also watered by the aid of lawn
sprinklers. A top-of-the-range product was the Pluviette
patent, which was capable of spraying water over quite a
large area. Although it looks like an early piece, these were
still popular in the 1930s.
£150–250/$225–375

▼ Various sprayers, 20th century
The largest of these is a pneumatic knapsack sprayer by Four
Oaks. It is made of a non-corrosive brass alloy for spraying
mixtures including lime sulphur. The pneumatic hand sprayer to
the left, possibly by Mysto c.1930, is copper with brass fittings.
£10–50/$15–75 (each)

◄ Water barrow, 1920s
The two-wheeled, swing water barrow
allowed water to be moved as well as stored,
and it sometimes also came with a pump.
Such barrows were popular in Victorian times,
and into the early 20th century, and limited
numbers recently have been reproduced.
£60–100/$90–150

TERRACOTTA & GLASS

Terracotta is a natural material for garden use, as it is fired clay, and it was particularly popular for various types of forcing pot from the mid-19th century to the middle of the 20th century. Sadly comparatively few flower pots are made in terracotta today but, in its heyday, pots of many specialized types were produced for plants such as orchids or alpines. Whereas forcing pots exclude light, the natural benefit of using light and heat to develop plants in glass bell jars or cloches is evident. These were particularly popular in France from the 18th century, and the name "cloche" reflects this: it is the French word for "bell" and the bell jars, or cloches, are manufactured in the shape of a bell.

FLOWER POTS & FORCING POTS

These were very often made by companies that also produced chimney pots, and other domestic fittings, over a wide area of Great Britain. Well-known companies that produced flower pots in particular are Sankys and The Royal Pottery, situated in Weston-super-Mare. Normally the sizes would vary between "Thimbles", which are 5cm (2in) in diameter and depth, and "Twos", which are 46cm (18in) in diameter and 36cm (14in) deep.

Forcing pots are still made by some specialist potteries today. However, there is a premium on antique stamped pieces, those with some decoration, and particularly those with intact original lids, as these have usually been lost or damaged in some way.

▲ Terracotta forcing pots
Forcing pots were commonly used in the 19th century to accelerate the growth of certain vegetables, and they are making a comeback today. There are principally two types: the taller example here, 58cm (23in) high, is for rhubarb and probably dates to c.1910; the shorter pot, 41cm (16in) high, is for sea kale and its condition suggests it is mid-Victorian. **£80–150/$120–225 (each)**

▶ Stamped flower pots, 20th century
Some flower pots have collectable appeal, particularly large ones that are stamped with the makers' names. The middle-sized pot here is stamped with a crowned "E.R.", as it was produced for the Coronation of Elizabeth II in 1953. **£2–10/$3–15 (each)**

▼ Glass bell jars (cloches)

These bell-shaped glass covers were highly popular in France from the 18th century. Many examples will date from the early 20th century, when they were used fairly extensively in nurseries. As glass is a material likely to break, it is not surprising to find that plastic cloches are now stocked by most modern garden centres.

£60–80/$90–120 (each)

▲ Handlight, late Victorian

Handlights are rather like miniature greenhouses. They have probably been around for a few hundred years, but you are unlikely to find one made much earlier than 1850. At that time a number of manufacturers of cast-iron started to produce frames that could be relatively easily glazed when repairs were necessary. There are numerous sizes and shapes available, and the late Victorian example shown above is one of the more common types. Reproductions are also produced today.

£100–150/$150–225

▶ More unusual items

There were many glass items for garden use that we might now regard as novelties. The scarce cucumber straightener was conceived in the 19th century at a time when a correctly shaped cucumber was required by the gardener for exhibition purposes. Another somewhat strange but practical item is the Copped Hall patent Grape Storage Bottle, c.1910–30, which facilitates the storage of a bunch of grapes by placing the stalk/stem in the neck of the bottle. The bottle was filled with water by means of a filling hole in the body.

Grape bottle: £20–30/$30–45
Cucumber straightener:
£80–120/$120–180
Miniature handlights: £10–15/
$15–23 (each)

MOWERS, ROLLERS, & BARROWS

Wheelbarrows evolved from hand barrows, and early rollers were made from stone. However, it was the invention of the lawn mower that was one of the greatest contributions to gardening and, in many ways, changed the focus towards leisure. At the beginning of the 19th century a lawn had to be cut with a scythe, and only a skilled man could prepare a piece of ground to make it suitable for some games or clear an area of grass for recreation. By the end of the century most householders with gardens could afford mowers, and create not only lawns but, given the space, also areas for tennis or croquet. This had a big impact on the social scene at that time, and also on the development of sport.

▶ **Chain-driven mower, Thomas Green, 1880s**
Thomas Green was one of the earliest manufacturers of mowers and this design was in production for decades, making it one of the most commonly encountered examples. This one was repainted blue (many years ago) and is shown with its original green grass box. The grass box is probably scarcer than the mower, since many are lost or damaged over time.
£60–100/$90–150

COLLECTING IMPLEMENTS

Obviously space and/or financial considerations must be taken into account. Large tools are not necessarily expensive, but may need more display space if the collector is to enjoy them. If you are just starting to collect garden implements, it would be best to try collecting a range of complementary items rather than simply trying to find as many examples of one item as possible, because that could prove more difficult and also more expensive.

▲ **Wheelbarrow, early 20th century**
This is an example of a garden barrow that could be purchased painted or unpainted. Good barrows are usually constructed of elm and ash and strengthened with iron supports. The presence of a wooden wheel tends to raise the value over that of later types, which were fitted with pneumatic tyres for wheels.
£80–120/$120–180

▲ **Roller, Shanks Arbroath, 19th century**
Garden rollers are rarely used today but are still useful and decorative. Owing to their robust construction many from the 19th century have survived; some of these have very attractive handles. Shanks Arbroath is probably better known for its lawn mowers, including pony-drawn versions for estates and golf courses, but this is a particularly decorative example of the sort of rollers the company made.
£50–80/$75–120

CARE & SECURITY

It would be unwise to ignore the increasing instances of theft from the garden. The market for garden ornament is strong, and the very fact that the value of the pieces in your garden has increased significantly over the last 20 years means that there is an increasing temptation for thieves to steal items.

Thankfully there are some good security devices available, and you should consider the initial outlay on security as money well spent. Increasingly, insurance companies have become unwilling to cover unprotected garden ornaments, and the money spent on security should be recouped by a decrease in premium.

The first thing you should do is to photograph all your garden ornaments, so that if the worst happens and an item is stolen you have a picture to give the police. Take good, close-up photographs and note the size of the piece on the back. You should also write on the photograph any other information that you may have on the piece. Mark your post-code on all your pieces with an ultra-violet pen, or any other tagging system. This will help the police return them to you if they are recovered. As most pieces of garden ornament are manufactured from the same moulds, it is useful to be able to identify your particular ornament. It is no use saying, after your bench has been stolen, that it was painted white, or blue, because it takes only half an hour for it to be repainted. Note any defects and identifying marks that appear under the paint.

Large pieces, such as statuary and fountains, should be tagged and, if possible, anchored into the ground. You can fit a screech alarm to these so that if someone tries to move them the alarm sounds. Do not think that something is too big to move: things have been craned over walls, and in one instance we have heard of a bronze fountain being removed from a garden in the South of France by a helicopter.

Be particularly careful with lead ornaments – the belief that lead is a valuable material is widespread, and they seem to attract thieves. Lead, in fact, is not particularly valuable as "scrap", but the old stories about stealing lead from church roofs are still with us.

The various security devices and identification processes are explained below – these will all help you to protect your property:

Trovan ID tags

These are invisible electronic tags, securely connected by being drilled into the items they protect. The police have 3,500 tag readers that can make instant identifications.

Uniquely powerful, the tags can be detected through almost any material – including dirt, wood, and several layers of paint. They are also weatherproof.

Garden Sitter

This system informs you as soon as anyone attempts to snatch or dig up something from your garden. The system consists of two main parts: sensors that are placed by the object to be protected, and a small mains-powered receiver. The receiver could be used in your kitchen during the day and moved to your bedroom at night. Any considerable movement around the sensors prompts them to trigger a quiet alarm in the receiver – enough to warn you but not the thieves. The sensors are 9 x 9cm (3½ x 3½in), durable, and waterproof. Their sensitivity is set before despatch, and they have a range of up to 60m (195ft).

Plant Anchor

This does exactly what its name suggests: the plant is held in place with flexible, adjustable threads that are drilled into the ground through the bottom of the plant pot. There are options for every surface, so you can use one on soft ground or a concrete patio. Once installed, the anchor is concealed so it won't impair the beauty of your plant and pot.

Microdots

A microdot is a tiny particle of polyester film, about the size of a grain of sand. It is comparable to commercial state-of-the-art microfilm and should last about 20 years.

A unique code is printed on each dot using an advanced micron laser-printing process. The dots are then coated with a thin protective film that resists abrasion, ultraviolet light, water, and most acids and solvents. They are particularly useful for ironwork, statuary, and for high-value machinery such as ride-on mowers that are otherwise "sanitized" or "de-identified" by thieves.

Lock Alarm

This is also referred to as a "screech alarm" and can be used to secure small items, shed doors, gates, and furniture. The cases of the locks are made from hardened steel, and tampering sets off flashing lights and a high-pitched noise.

Failing all these, perhaps you should consider the protection value of a large noisy dog!

DIRECTORY OF MAKERS

This is by no means an exhaustive list of every manufacturer of garden ornament, but what it does do is highlight many of the principal names and firms to look out for.

Austin & Seeley

Active 1828 to the late 19th century. One of the foremost English manufacturers of composition stone garden ornament. *See* box on page 82.

F. Barbedienne

Active *c.*1850–95. A French foundry producing cast iron, bronze, and brass, but which also carved in marble. The firm employed notable sculptors, such as Bayre and David. It also had the sole rights to the Collas sculpture-reduction technique.

Barbezat et Cie

A French foundry that was eventually incorporated into the Val d'Osne group *c.*1857.

Barnard, Bishop and Barnard

English metalworkers and iron founders. The firm is particularly noted for its revolving summer houses, which it made during the early part of the 20th century.

Mark H. Blanchard

Active 1839–70. English terracotta manufacturer who bought many of Coade's moulds when it ceased trading. *See* box on page 84.

John Merriott Blashfield

Active 1830–75. English manufacturer of terracotta architectural and garden ornament. The company also bought some of Coade's moulds, and employed the sculptor John Bell in 1854.

Boulton & Paul

Founded in 1797. Based in Norfolk, this iron foundry started making summer houses between the two world wars. *See* box on page 111.

The Bromsgrove Guild

1898–1966. English firm founded by the sculptor Walter Gilbert, who assembled a group of artists to produce a wide variety of wares, from lead garden ornament to stained glass and gates. Its most notable commission was the iron and bronze gates of Buckingham Palace. *See* box on page 31.

Henry and Julius Caesar

An early 20th-century English firm of house builders that also made rustic summer houses.

James W. Carr

Active during the 19th century. This American firm of iron founders shifted production from artillery to garden ornament, including a fern-pattern seat that resembles, but is not identical to, the Coalbrookdale Fern and Blackberry seat (*see* page 68).

Carron

Founded in 1759. Scottish iron foundry originally involved in armaments, but moved to making domestic cast iron as well. John Adam (a relation of Robert Carron) became a partner in 1765.

Chiurrazzi

Italian firm that produced a vast number of copies of Roman antiques in bronze, iron, and marble.

Coade

Active 1769–1842. English manufacturer of stoneware. Unusual in that it was the first firm to produce stoneware for garden and architectural ornament, its stated aim being to make fired clay that would withstand the English climate, and would look identical to carved stone. It is worth noting that the firm was founded and run by a woman, Eleanor Coade, at a time when there were very few women in business. *See* box on page 40.

Coalbrookdale

1708–1996. English iron foundry that progressed from the production of domestic ironwork to designing and producing a variety of architectural and garden ornament. *See* box on page 64.

Compton Pottery

1896–1950s. Also known as the Potters Arts Guild. English manufacturers of terracotta garden ornament. *See* box on page 28.

J. and M. Craig

Founded 1831 and closed in 1914. Scottish fireclay manufacturer.

Doulton

Active 1820–1956. English ceramics company. *See* box on page 41.

J.J. Ducel et Fils

Early 19th century–1930s. French iron and bronze foundry that joined the Val d'Osne Foundry and produced statuary and urns in profusion.

Antoine Durenne

Active 1847–1930s. French iron and bronze foundry that joined Val d'Osne.

Falkirk Iron Company

Active during the 19th century. Scottish iron foundry.

Fiske Foundry

Founded in 1858 and closed in 1933. American iron foundry. *See* box on page 42.

Garnkirk Fireclay Company

Founded in 1832 and closed in 1901. Scottish manufacturer of fireclay urns and fountains.

Gaskell and Chambers

Active late 19th century to second half of the 20th century. English iron foundry that was particularly associated with the manufacture of "pub" tables.

Grangemouth Fireclay Works

Active in the 19th and 20th centuries. Scottish exhibitor in the 1851 Great Exhibition; produced a large range of garden ornament.

Handyside Foundry

Founded in 1848, when Andrew Handyside bought the Britannia Iron Works. English firm of iron founders well known for its fountains and urns. *See* box on page 45.

George Jennings

Founded in 1860 and closed in 1910. English pottery based in Poole, whose work was predominantly of an architectural nature.

Kenrick and Son

Active 1795 to present. English iron foundry that produces a range of cast-iron garden ornament, including some of Coalbrookdale's own designs.

Augustus Kiss

Active during the mid-19th century. German manufacturer of zinc copies of contemporary sculpture.

LEFCO

Acronym of the Leeds Fireclay Company, which has been active since the mid-19th century. English fireclay manufacturers whose distinctive Art Nouveau style glazed ceramics also went under the trade name of "Burmantofts". *See* box on page 54

Liberty and Co.

Active since 1875. English decorative arts retailer that had numerous garden ornaments produced by the Compton Pottery. *See* box on page 27.

Walter Macfarlane and Co.

Active 1852–1979. Scottish iron foundry that produced mainly architectural works, but also some cast-iron garden ornament.

Manifattura di Signa

Active since late 19th century. Italian terracotta manufacturers that produce many designs after, or inspired by, the antique.

Miroy Frères

Active during the late 19th century. French zinc and spelter foundry.

J.L. Mott & Co.

Active since 1828. American iron foundry originally based in New York, now in New Jersey. *See* box on page 71.

Pulham Terracotta

Active *c.*1806–1945. English manufacturer of numerous garden ornaments. Also made "Pulhamite" – artificial stones that were used for manufacturing grottoes and water-courses; these can be seen at Compton Acres, Waddesdon Manor, and Batsford Arboretum, among other places.

James Stiff and Sons

Active 1876 to the early 20th century. English stoneware manufacturer producing a range of garden ornament in Lambeth.

Peter Timmes and Sons

Active 1860–1903. American iron foundry based in Brooklyn.

Val d'Osne

Active 1840–1910. French iron and bronze foundry. The Société Anonyme des Haute-Fourneaux et Fonderies du Val d'Osne was a collective of the foundries in the Haute Marne department of France, and included Barbezat, Ducel, and Durenne. A very large variety of garden ornaments and architectural designs was produced.

James Yates

Active 1840–70. English iron foundry that became Yates and Hayward in 1851. Best known for its Gothic-pattern furniture.

CLASSICAL ICONOGRAPHY

Abundance
Principal attribute the cornucopia (horn of plenty); sometimes several children or a sheaf of corn, as her prototype was Ceres. Also sometimes a rudder from the Roman celebration of the grain harvest.

Adam and Eve
Normally naked, with hands covering their pudenda. Eve may also be offering Adam an apple.

Aeolus
God of the winds, most commonly seen on the base of Giam Bologna's Mercury, supporting him on a jet of air.

Amazon
Legendary race of warrior women, normally depicted with one bare breast and carrying weapons.

Anchor
Attribute of Hope personified.

Apollo
One of the 12 Olympian gods who stood for man's rational and civilized side. Many attributes: a lyre, a bow or quiver, a laurel wreath, or a snake.

Aratino
Name of a Roman sculpture of the man who flayed Marsyas; he is usually depicted sharpening his knife.

Artemis
See Diana (Roman).

Aphrodite
See Venus (Roman).

Atalanta and Hippomenes
Atalanta was an athletic huntress who raced suitors, Hippomenes won by dropping golden apples that Atalanta picked up, thus slowing her down. She is normally depicted picking up an apple.

Atlas
A Titan who is depicted supporting the world on his head and hands.

Bacchus (Greek: Dionysus)
One of the 12 Olympian gods, and the god of wine. Attributes include a wreath of vine leaves or grapes, sometimes a drinking cup, and a thyrsus – a wand tipped with a pine cone that was an ancient fertility symbol.

Bacchante
Female follower of Bacchus.

Boar
Symbol of Lust personified.

Boreas
The north wind and, in the Seasons, represents Winter.

Bridle
Attribute of Temperance, Nemesis, and Fortune.

Butterfly wings
These are an attribute of Zephyr, the husband of Flora.

Caduceus
This emblem of the messenger – normally Mercury – is a winged wand entwined with snakes.

Caiman
A crocodile-like reptile that is one of the attributes of America.

Cards
Associated with Vice personified.

Centaur
One of a mythical race of half-human, half-horse beings that populated Thessaly in Greece.

Cerberus
The many-headed dog who guarded the entrance to the underworld.

Ceres
Goddess of agriculture, normally associated with a sheaf of corn, a sickle, or a cornucopia; also has ears of corn tucked behind her own.

Chastity
May wear a veil, and hold a palm frond.

Cleopatra
Normally depicted with a snake entwined around her forearm.

Compasses
Attribute of Astronomy and Urania, one of the Muses.

Continents (figures representing)
Europe: depicted with a crown, and holding a sceptre with a model of a temple; her animal is a horse. Asia: depicted with a crown of flowers holding a censer and a palm; her animal is a camel. Africa: depicted with black skin, wearing a coral necklace and holding a scorpion; her animals are a lion and a snake. North America: depicted in a feather headdress, holding a bow and arrow; her animal is a caiman.

Cronus
Father Time, or Saturn, with an hourglass.

Crow
Attribute of Hope personified.

Cupid (Greek: Eros/Roman: Amor)
God of love, often a winged youth
and blindfolded.

David
King of Israel, often depicted with a sling.

Diana (Greek: Artemis)
Roman goddess first associated with
chastity. Depicted as a huntress in
short tunic with her hair tied back
and either a spear or bow and arrows.

Dice
Symbol of fortune.

Eagle
Attribute of Jupiter, also sometimes
shown with a thunderbolt in its beak.

Fasces
Bundle of reeds with an axe head,
symbol of Justice.

Father Time
Often depicted with a sickle and
hourglass. *See* Cronus.

Fig
Associated with Adam and Eve
in same way that an apple is.

Fleece
If flat, with a warrior kneeling by, it is
a symbol of Gideon; if hanging it is a
symbol of the golden fleece and Jason.

Flora
Roman goddess of flowers
whose attributes are flowers.

Flowers
In general, attributes of Flora and Spring.

Ganymede
A shepherd boy of deep beauty whom
Zeus fell in love with; he was carried

away by Zeus in the form of an eagle.
Often depicted with an eagle or a dog.

Goat
A symbol of lust or the damned; also
associated with the worship of Bacchus.

Gorgons
Three sisters of hideous aspect, with
snakes for hair and glaring eyes.

Griffin
A mythical creature with the head,
wings, and claws of an eagle, and the
body of a lion.

Hare
Symbol of lust, along with the rabbit.

Hercules
A hero, and personification of strength
and courage; often depicted with a club
and dressed in a lion skin.

Herm
An armless torso of a god supported
on a rectangular plinth, originally
thought to be the god Hermes.

Hermes
See Mercury.

Hippocampus
Mythical sea creature with the fore-parts
of a horse and the rear of a fish.

Hourglass
Symbol of Father Time and Death.

Ivy
Sacred to Bacchus, and a symbol
of his attendant satyrs.

Janus
Roman god of doorways and entrances;
depicted with a face on each side of his
head, so he can look both ways.

Juno
Chief goddess on Olympus whose
sacred animal was the peacock; also
both sister and wife of Jupiter.

Jupiter (Greek: Zeus)
Supreme ruler of the gods, depicted
as an eagle or with thunderbolts.

Laurel
Attribute of Apollo; if a woman is
holding some laurel she is Daphne (a
nymph chased by Apollo). It is also a
symbol of literature and the arts.

Leopard
Sacred to Bacchus, who is sometimes
shown in a chariot drawn by two leopards.

Lily
Symbol of purity, associated
with the Virgin Mary.

Lizard
Attribute of Logic personified.

Loom
Associated with Penelope, who whiled
away the time that Odysseus (Ulysses)
was away by constantly weaving and
re-weaving the same piece of cloth.

Lute
Associated with Music personified;
also with Hearing, with Polyhymnia
(one of the Muses), and with Apollo.

Lyre
Also associated with Apollo.

Maenad
See Bacchante.

Mars (Greek: Aries)
God of war, normally depicted wearing
a helmet, and holding a shield and
a sword or spear.

Mercury (Greek: Hermes)

One of the 12 gods of Olympus, often depicted with a winged helmet, or winged shoes, and a caduceus. Messenger of the gods, and their guide.

Minerva (Greek: Athena)

One of the 12 Olympian gods. Similar to Apollo in that she was benevolent and civilizing. Attributes normally a shield, a spear, and armour.

Mirror

Associated with Prudence, Pride, Vanity, Lust, and Sight.

Naiads

The nymphs of fresh waters.

Narcissus

Often depicted leaning over a pool, with narcissi sprouting at his feet.

Neptune (Greek: Poseidon)

God of the sea, often depicted with a net, or sea creatures, and a trident.

Nereids

Attendants of Poseidon, most often depicted with tridents or sea items.

Night

Often depicted floating in the sky; her attributes include stars and poppies.

Nymph – Echo

The nymph who fell in love with Narcissus, often depicted with a hand cupped to her ear, or calling out.

Orpheus

Legendary Greek poet who is most commonly depicted with a lute.

Owl

Associated with Minerva, goddess of wisdom.

Pan

Greek god of flocks and herds, woods and fields. His attributes are the legs of a goat, a goat-like face, pointed ears, and horns, and he is commonly shown playing pipes.

Pegasus

Winged horse of Greek mythology, who sprang from the neck of Medusa when Perseus cut off her head.

Penelope

Wife of Odysseus (Ulysses), who put off her suitors by continuously weaving and undoing a shroud for her father-in-law. She is normally depicted weaving or spinning yarn.

Purse

Attribute of Mercury, who is often seen as the god of commerce.

Satyrs

Attendants of Bacchus: hence they are depicted with goat legs, horns, and bearded faces, and often with tails too.

Scales

An attribute of Justice personified.

Seasons

Spring: depicted holding flowers.
Summer: depicted holding a sickle and/or a sheaf of corn.
Autumn: depicted holding grapes and vine leaves.
Winter: depicted warmly dressed and holding a flaming torch. See Boreas.

Silenus

Also an attendant of Bacchus, but depicted as a fat, old, drunken man.

Snake/Serpent

Has many connotations: evil, fertility, wisdom, and the power to heal.

Sphinx

An Egyptian symbol of power, depicted as a lion with a human head. However, the Greeks portrayed the sphinx with a female head, and breasts.

Sunflowers

Symbol of Clytie, whose jealousy caused her to waste away into a sunflower.

Theseus

Legendary Greek hero, who is most famed for, and most commonly depicted as, struggling with the Minotaur.

Minotaur

Mythical half-man, half-bull creature from Greek legend.

Torch

Has numerous connotations: can be the attribute of Ceres (while she searches for Proserpine), or symbolize the fire of passion, if held by Cupid or Venus.

Triton

Son of Neptune, depicted as half-man, half-fish.

Veil

The attribute of Chastity personified.

Venus (Greek: Aphrodite)

Goddess of love and fertility; numerous attributes, including a pair of doves or swans, dolphins, scallop shell, and the myrtle. There are many antique and Renaissance Venus statues.

Wolves

These animals were sacred to Apollo and Mars, and are also associated with Romulus and Remus (the founding brothers of Rome).

Zeus

See Jupiter (Roman).

FURTHER READING

Atterbury, Paul & Irvine, Louise
The Doulton Story
(souvenir booklet for the exhibition
held at the Victoria and Albert
Museum, London, 30 May–12
August 1979)

Davis, John
Antique Garden Ornaments
(Antique Collectors' Club, 1991)

Dunn, Teri
Garden Antiques & Collectibles
(Friedman/Fairfax Publishing, 1999)

Franklin Gould, Veronica
The Watts Chapel: An Arts & Crafts Memorial
(Arrow Press, 1993)

Haskell, Francis & Nicholas
Taste and the Antique
(York University Press, 1998)

Hudson, Norman
Hudson's Historic Houses and Gardens
(Norman Hudson & Co.,
annual publication)

Huxley, Anthony
Illustrated History of Gardening
(Macmillan, 1978)

Israel, Barbara
Antique Garden Ornament, Two Centuries of American Taste
(Harry N. Abrams, Inc, 1999)

Jekyll, Gertrude
Garden Ornament
(Antique Collectors' Club, 1982,
2nd ed.)

Kelly, Alison
Mrs Coade's Stone
(The Self Publishing Association
Ltd, 1990)

Lablaude, Pierre A.
The Gardens of Versailles
(Sotheby's Publications, 1994)

Morris, Alistair
Antiques from the Garden
(Garden Art Press, 2001,
new ed.)

Picas, Stephane & Gilotte
Maryvonne Versailles
(Thames & Hudson, 1996)

Plumtre, George
Garden Ornament
(Thames and Hudson, 1989)

Sanecki, Kay N.
Old Garden Tools
(Shire Publications, 1997)

Slesin, Suzanne, et al
Garden Tools
(Abbeville Press, 1996)

Weaver, Lawrence
English Leadwork
(Benjamin Blom, 1972, new ed.)

Yellin Outwater, Myra
Antique Garden Tools & Accessories
(Schiffer Publishing, 2002)

**Yellin Outwater, Myra
& Outwater, Eric B.**
Garden Ornaments & Antiques
(Schiffer Publishing, 2000)

WHERE TO BUY & SEE

PLACES TO BUY

UK

Auction Houses

Thomas Gaze and Sons
Roydon Road,
Diss,
Norfolk IP22 4LN
Telephone 01379 650306

Sotheby's
Summers Place,
Billingshurst,
West Sussex RH14 9AD
Telephone 01403 833500
(only major auction house to have
specialist sales of garden statuary)

Specialist Dealers & Manufacturers

The Architectural Emporium
The Bald Faced Stag,
Ashurst, Tunbridge Wells,
Kent TN3 9TE
Telephone 01892 740877

Architectural Heritage
Taddington Manor,
Taddington, Temple Guiting,
Cheltenham GL54 5RY
Telephone 01386 584414

Nigel Bartlett
25 St Barnabas Street,
London SW1W 8QB
Telephone 020 7730 3223
(specialists in chimney pieces)

Chilstone
Victoria Park,
Fordcombe Road,
Langton Green,
Tunbridge Wells,
Kent TN3 0RE
Telephone 01892 740866
(manufacturers and retailers of
modern composition-stone ornament)

Cotswold Decorative Ironwork
Marsh Farm,
Stourton,
Warwickshire CV36 5HG
Telephone 01608 685134
(specialists in modern wrought-
and cast-iron decoration)

The Country Seat
Huntercombe Manor Barn,
Henley-on-Thames,
Oxfordshire RG9 5RY
Telephone 01491 641349
(garden ornament and furniture)

H. Crowther
5 The High Road,
Chiswick,
London W4 2ND
Telephone 020 8994 2326
(producer of modern leadwork)

Drummonds
The Kirkpatrick Buildings,
25 London Road,
Hindhead,
Surrey GU26 6AB
Telephone 01428 609444
(specialists in garden ornament, and
architectural salvage and decoration)

Elliot and Snowdon
20 Mexfield Road,
London SW15 2RQ
Telephone 020 8874 3139

Flaxton Antique Gardens
Glebe Farm,
Flaxton,
York YO60 7RU
Telephone 01904 468468

Haddonstone
The Forge House,
East Haddon,
Northamptonshire NN6 8DP
Telephone 01604 770711
(manufacturers and retailers of modern
composition-stone ornament)

Holloway's
Lower Court,
Church Lane,
Suckley,
Worcester WR6 5DE
Telephone 01886 884 665

Jardinique
Old Park Farm,
Beech,
nr Alton,
Hampshire GU34 4AW
Telephone 01420 560005

LASSCO St Michael's
Mark Street,
London EC2A 4ER
Telephone 020 7749 9944
(architectural salvage)

Pew Corner
Artington Manor Farm,
Old Portsmouth Road,
Guildford,
Surrey GU3 1LP
Telephone 01483 533337
(specialists in recycled church
furnishings, pews, grilles, and doors)

Reclamation Services
Catbrain Quarry,
Painswick Beacon,
nr Stroud,
Gloucestershire GL6 6SU
Telephone 01452 814064
(specialists in reclaimed
architectural pieces)

Sweerts de Landas
Dunsborough Park,
Ripley, Woking,
Surrey GU23 6AL
Telephone 01483 225366
(garden ornament – please ring
for an appointment)

**Woodlands Farm Nursery
and Reclamation**
The Green,
Wood Street Village,
Guildford,
Surrey GU3 3DU
Telephone 01483 235536

Antiques Fairs
Olympia Fine Art and Antiques Fair
Olympia Exhibition Centre
Hammersmith Road,
London W14
Telephone 020 7370 8234
www.olympia-antiques.co.uk/FAAF
(Feb/March, June and Nov every year)

Grosvenor House Antiques Fair
Grosvenor House,
86–90 Park Lane, London W1A 3AA
Telephone 020 7399 8100
www.grosvenor-antiquesfair.co.uk
(June every year)

LAPADA Antiques and Fine Art Fair
National Exhibition Centre
Birmingham B40 1NT
(Jan every year)
and
Commonwealth Institute Galleries
Kensington High Street,
London W8 6NQ
(every October)
Telephone 0121 767 2760
www.lapada.co.uk/fairs

USA
Specialist Dealers
Finnegan Gallery
2030 North Mohawk Street,
Chicago,
IL 60614-4537
Telephone 773 235 1573

Barbara Israel Garden Antiques
Mount Holly Road,
Katonah,
NY 10536
Telephone 212 249 1377

PLACES TO VISIT

UK

Garden Furniture and Sculpture
The National Trust (www.nationaltrust.org.uk)
owns many houses and gardens that
include decorative sculpture and urns,
including the following:

Anglesey Abbey
Lode,
Cambridgeshire CB5 9EJ
Telephone 01223 811200

Fountains Abbey & Studley Royal
Ripon,
Yorkshire HG4 3DY
Telephone 01765 608888
www.fountainsabbey.org.uk

Ham House
Ham,
Richmond,
Surrey TW10 7RS
Telephone 020 8940 1950

Hanbury Hall
Droitwich,
Worcestershire WR9 7EA
Telephone 01527 821214

Mount Stewart
Newtownards,
Co. Down BT22 2AD
Northern Ireland
Telephone 028 4278 8387

Petworth House & Park
Petworth,
West Sussex GU28 0AE
Telephone 01798 342207/343929

Stourhead
Stourton,
Warminster,
Wiltshire BA12 6QD
Telephone 01747 841152

Stowe Landscape Garden
Stowe,
Buckinghamshire MK18 5EH
Telephone 01280 822850

Waddesdon Manor
Waddesdon,
nr Aylesbury,
Buckinghamshire HP18 0JH
Telephone 01296 653203
www.waddesdon.org.uk

West Wycombe Park
West Wycombe,
Buckinghamshire HP14 3AJ
Telephone 01494 513569

Non-National Trust Properties:

Belvoir Castle
Belvoir,
Grantham,
Leicestershire NG32 1PD
Telephone 01476 871000
www.belvoircastle.com

Blenheim Palace
Woodstock,
Oxon OX20 1PX
Telephone 01993 811091
www.blenheimpalace.com

Bolsover Castle
Castle Street,
Bolsover,
Derbyshire S44 6PR
Telephone 01246 822844
www.english-heritage.org.uk

Bowood House
Derry Hill,
Calne,
Wiltshire SN11 9PQ
Telephone 01249 812102
www.bowood-house.org

Broughton Hall
Skipton,
North Yorkshire BD23 3AE
Telephone 01756 799608
www.broughtonhall.co.uk

Castle Howard
York,
North Yorkshire YO60 7DA
Telephone 01653 648444
www.castlehoward.co.uk

Chatsworth
Bakewell,
Derbyshire DE45 1PP
Telephone 01246 565300
www.chatsworth-house.co.uk

Chiswick House
Burlington Lane,
Chiswick,
London W4 2RP
Telephone 020 8995 0508

Cobham Hall
Cobham,
Kent DA12 3BL
Telephone 01474 824319

Corsham Court
Corsham,
Wiltshire SN13 0BZ
Telephone 01249 701610
www.corsham-court.co.uk

Drummond Castle Gardens
Muthill, Crieff,
Perthshire, PH5 2AA
Telephone 01764 681257

Hampton Court Palace
Surrey KT8 9AU
Telephone 0870 752 7777
www.hrp.org.uk/webcode/
hampton_home.asp

Hever Castle
Edenbridge,
Kent TN8 7NG
Telephone 01732 865224
www.hevercastle.co.uk

The Peto Garden at Iford Manor
Bradford-on-Avon,
Wiltshire BA15 2BA
Telephone 01225 863146
www.ifordmanor.co.uk

Kensington Gardens
Park Office,
Magazine Gate,
London W2 2UH
Telephone 020 7298 2100
www.royalparks.gov.uk/kensington.htm

Melbourne Hall
Melbourne,
Derbyshire DE73 1EN
Telephone 01332 862502
www.derbyshireuk.net/
melbourne_hall.html

Osborne House
Osborne House Estate,
East Cowes,
Isle of Wight PO32 6JX
Telephone 01983 200022

Painshill Park
Portsmouth Road,
Cobham,
Surrey KT11 1JE
Telephone 01932 864674
www.painshill.co.uk

Parham House & Gardens
nr Pulborough,
West Sussex RH20 4HS
Telephone 01903 742021
www.parhaminsussex.co.uk

Shugborough Hall
Milford,
nr Stafford ST17 0XB
Telephone 01889 881388

Somerleyton Hall & Gardens
Somerleyton,
Lowestoft,
Suffolk NR32 5QQ
Telephone 01502 730224
www.somerleyton.co.uk

Syon House
Syon Park,
Brentford,
Middlesex TW8 8JF
Telephone 020 8560 0881
www.syonpark.co.uk

Wilton House
Wilton, nr Salisbury,
Wiltshire SP2 0BJ
Telephone 01722 746720
www.wiltonhouse.co.uk

Witley Court
Great Witley,
Worcestershire WR6 6JT
Telephone 01299 896636

Wrest Park Gardens
Silsoe,
nr Luton,
Bedfordshire MK45 4HS
Telephone 01525 860152

Victoria and Albert Museum
Cromwell Road, South Kensington,
London SW7 2RL
Telephone 020 7942 2000
www.vam.ac.uk/

Modern Sculpture

Hannah Pescher Sculpture Garden
Black and White Cottage,
Standon Lane, Ockley,
Surrey RH5 5QR
Telephone 01306 627269

Sculpture at Goodwood
Goodwood House,
Chichester,
West Sussex PO18 0QF
Telephone 01243 538449
www.sculpture.org.uk
(includes modern and contemporary
sculptors such as Dame Elisabeth Frink)

**Barbara Hepworth Museum
& Sculpture Garden**
Barnoon Hill, St. Ives,
Cornwall TR26 1AD
Telephone 01736 796226
www.tate.org.uk/stives/hepworth

Royal Horticultural Society
Flower Shows

These will not include antique ornament,
but have a collection of "show" gardens
that give ideas of how to use ornament:

Chelsea Flower Show
Royal Hospital, Chelsea,
Royal Hospital Road,
London SW3 4SR
Telephone 0870 906 3781
(annual show in May)

Hampton Court Palace Flower Show
Surrey KT8 9AN
Telephone 0870 906 3791
(annual show in July)

Cast-iron Ornament

The Ironbridge Gorge Museums
Ironbridge,
Telford,
Shropshire TF8 7AW
Telephone 01952 432166
www.ironbridge.org.uk
(Coalbrookdale cast-iron furniture and
ornament, as well as the opportunity to
look at the famous Iron Bridge)

Garden Implements and Accessories

British Lawnmower Museum
106–114 Shakespeare Street,
Southport, Lancashire PR8 5AJ
Telephone 01704 501336
www.lawnmowerworld.co.uk

Halford Lawnmower Collection
Trerice Manor, nr Newquay
Cornwall TR8 4PG
Telephone 01637 875404

Museum of Garden History
St Mary's at Lambeth,
Lambeth Palace Road,
London SE1 7LB
Telephone 020 7401 8865
www.museumgardenhistory.org

Museum of London
London Wall,
London EC2Y 5HN
Telephone 020 7600 3699
www.museum-london.org.uk

National Museum of Gardening
Trevarno Manor,
Trevarno Estate, Helston,
Cornwall TR13 0RU
Telephone 01326 574274
www.trevarnoestateandgardens.co.uk

Weald & Downland Open Air Museum
Singleton, Chichester,
Sussex PO18 0EU
Telephone 01243 811363
www.wealddown.co.uk
(historic buildings; collections of country
crafts, trades, and agriculture)

USA

Garden Antiques in Historic Gardens

Belmont Mansion
1900 Belmont Boulevard,
Nashville, TN 37212
Telephone 615 460 5459
www.belmontmansion.com
(largest USA cast-iron ornament collection)

Biltmore Estate
One North Pack Square,
Asheville,
NC 28801
Telephone 828 225 1333
www.biltmore.com

Cliveden
6401 Germantown Avenue,
Philadelphia,
PA 19144
Telephone 215 848 1777
www.cliveden.org

Cranbrook House and Gardens
380 Lone Pine Road,
Bloomfield Hills,
MI 48303-0801
Telephone 248 645 3147
www.cranbrook.edu

Dumbarton Oaks
1703 32nd Street NW,
Washington, DC 20007
Telephone 202 339 6401
www.doaks.org

Hearst Castle
750 Hearst Castle Road,
San Simeon,
CA 93452-9741
Telephone 805 927 2020
www.hearstcastle.org

Kykuit (Historic Hudson Valley)
150 White Plains Road,
Tarrytown, NY 10591
Telephone 914 631 9491

Longwood Gardens
Route 1, PO Box 501,
Kennett Square,
PA 19348-0501
Telephone 610 388 1000
www.longwoodgardens.org

Maymont
1700 Hampton Street,
Richmond, VA 23220
Telephone 804 358 7166
www.maymont.org

Nemours Mansion and Gardens
1600 Rockland Road,
Wilmington,
DE 19899
Telephone 302 651 6912
www.nemours.org/no/ni/est/index.html

Old Westbury Gardens
71 Old Westbury Road,
Old Westbury, NY 11568
Telephone 516 333 0048
www.oldwestburygardens.org

Stan Hywet Hall and Gardens
714 North Portage Path,
Akron, OH 44303
Telephone 330 836 5533
www.stanhywet.org

Vanderbilt Mansion
4097 Albany Post Road,
Hyde Park,
NY 12538
Telephone 845 229 9115
www.nps.gov/vama

INDEX

Page numbers in *italics* refer to illustrations; those in **bold** refer to main entries.

ACKNOWLEDGMENTS

The authors would like to record their appreciation for the invaluable help of Alistair Morris FRICS, FRSA, of Sothebys, and Hilary Soper for their contribution to the chapter on Implements and Accessories; to Glynn Clarkson for his wonderful photographs; to Jo Dinsdale for her help in research; and to Alan and Mr Stripey for their encouragement at all times. We would also like to thank Emily Anderson of Mitchell Beazley for her patience and perseverence.

All pictures have been supplied courtesy of Sotheby's, Sussex, with the exception of the following:

Back cover: t OPG/GC/S, b S&OM

2 HGL/PW; **6** HGL/JH/CM; **8** all OPG/GC/S; **9** all OPG/GC/S; **10** all OPG/GC/S; **11** all OPG/GC/S; **12** S&OM; **14** r OPG/GC/S; **16** b OPG/JR; **20** l OPG/RVDW/S; **25** br AL; **27** tr OPG/GC/S; **29** r OPB/GC/S; **35** tr OPG/GC/S, b OPG/GC/S; **36** S&OM; **40** l OPG/GC/S; **41** tr OPG/GC/S; **46** c OPG/GC/S; **54** b OPG/GC/S; **56** ALP/MO; **64** t OPG/GC/S; **65** l OPG/AP; **72** b OPG/S; **76** AL; **83** l OPG/GC/S; **84** b OPG/GC/S; **92-93** all OPG/VS; **94** W&DOAM; **99** tl & tr OPG/JR; **99** cr OPG/JR; **101** tl & tr OPG/GC/S; **101** c OPG/GC/S; **102** HGL/MH; **105** br AL; **109** t OPG/GC/S, b GM/SS; **113** r OPG/GC/S; **114-123** all OPG/GC/AM; **125-128** all OPG/GC/AM; **129** tl & tr OPG/GC/AM, b OPG/RVDW/S

Key: b bottom, c centre, l left, r right, t top

AL Andrew Lawson
ALP/MO Andrew Lawson Photography/Mirabel Osler
GM/SS Garden Matters/Steffe Shields
HGL/JH/CM Harpur Garden Library/Jerry Harpur/Christopher Masson
HGL/MH Harpur Garden Library/Marcus Harpur
HGL//PW Harpur Garden Library/Peter Wooster
OPG/AP Octopus Publishing Group Ltd/Amanda Patton
OPG/GC/AM Octopus Publishing Group Ltd/Glynn Clarkson/Alastair Morris
OPG/GC/S Octopus Publishing Group Ltd/Glynn Clarkson/Sotheby's, Sussex
OPG/JR Octopus Publishing Group Ltd/Jackie Rees
OPG/RVDW/S Octopus Publishing Group Ltd/Rupert van der Werff/Sotheby's, Sussex
OPG/S Octopus Publishing Group Ltd/Sotheby's Sussex
OPG/VS Octopus Publishing Group Ltd/Vicky Short
S&OM S. & O. Mathews
W&DOAM Weald & Downland Open Air Museum